HIDING FROM THE NAZIS IN PLAIN SIGHT

A GRAPHIC NOVEL BIOGRAPHY OF
ZHANNA AND FRINA ARSHANSKAYA

WRITTEN BY LYDIA LUKIDIS   ILLUSTRATED BY ALEKSANDAR SOTIROVSKI

CAPSTONE PRESS
a capstone imprint

Published by Capstone Press, an imprint of Capstone
1710 Roe Crest Drive, North Mankato, Minnesota 56003
capstonepub.com

Library of Congress Cataloging-in-Publication Data
Names: Lukidis, Lydia, author. | Sotirovski, Aleksandar, illustrator.
Title: Hiding from the Nazis in plain sight : a graphic novel biography of Zhanna and Frina Arshanskaya / by Lydia Lukidis ; illustrated by Aleksandar Sotirovski.
Description: North Mankato : Capstone Press, 2024. | Series: Barrier breakers | Includes bibliographical references. | Audience: Ages 8-11 | Audience: Grades 4-6 | Summary: "Zhanna and Frina Arshanskaya were two talented child musicians when Nazis invaded their city of Kharkiv, Ukraine, during World War II. Along with their parents, the Jewish sisters were forced into a death march. They each eventually escaped and were reunited, but how would they survive the rest of the war? By hiding their true identities and becoming musical entertainment for German soldiers. Learn about their story of survival in this inspiring graphic novel"— Provided by publisher.
Identifiers: LCCN 2023018989 (print) | LCCN 2023018990 (ebook) | ISBN 9781669061779 (hardcover) | ISBN 9781669062004 (paperback) | ISBN 9781669061816 (pdf) | ISBN 9781669062028 (kindle edition) | ISBN 9781669062011 (epub)
Subjects: LCSH: Dawson, Zhanna—Juvenile literature. | Boldt, Frina—Juvenile literature. | Pianists—Biography—Juvenile literature. | Pianists—Biography—Comic books, strips, etc. | Jewish musicians—Biography—Juvenile literature. | Jewish musicians—Biography—Comic books, strips, etc. | Holocaust, Jewish (1939-1945)—Personal narratives—Juvenile literature. | Holocaust, Jewish (1939-1945)—Personal narratives—Comic books, strips, etc. | LCGFT: Biographies. | Biographical comics. | Educational comics.
Classification: LCC ML397 .L85 2024 (print) | LCC ML397 (ebook) | DDC 786.2092/2 [B]—dc23/eng/20230621
LC record available at https://lccn.loc.gov/2023018989
LC ebook record available at https://lccn.loc.gov/2023018990

Editorial Credits
Editor: Julie Gassman; Designer: Dina Her; Production Specialist: Tori Abraham

Editorial note: This book uses the preferred Ukrainian spelling of *Kharkiv* in support of the Ukrainian Ministry of Foreign Affairs. Historically, the city's name was often spelled *Kharkov,* as derived from the Russian spelling.

Printed and bound in the USA. 5626

TABLE OF CONTENTS

Piano Dreams

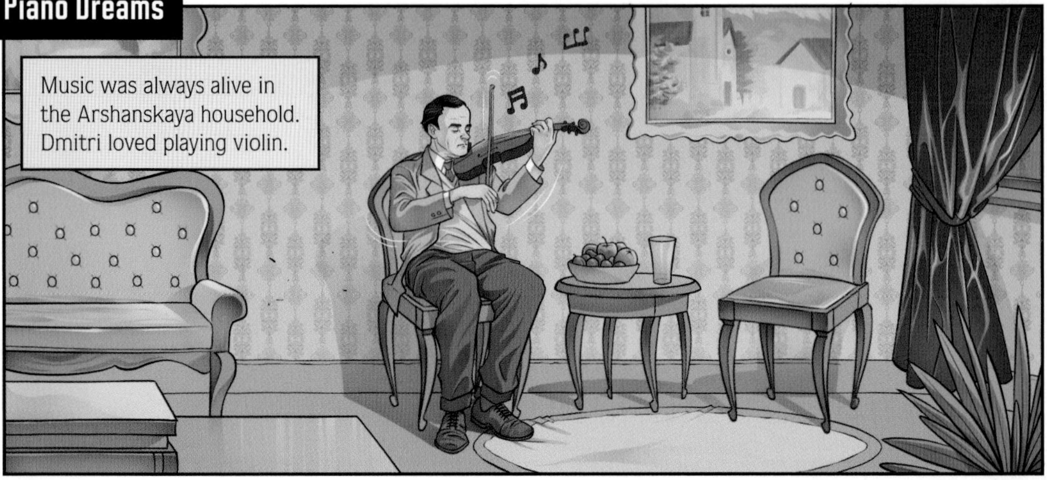
Music was always alive in the Arshanskaya household. Dmitri loved playing violin.

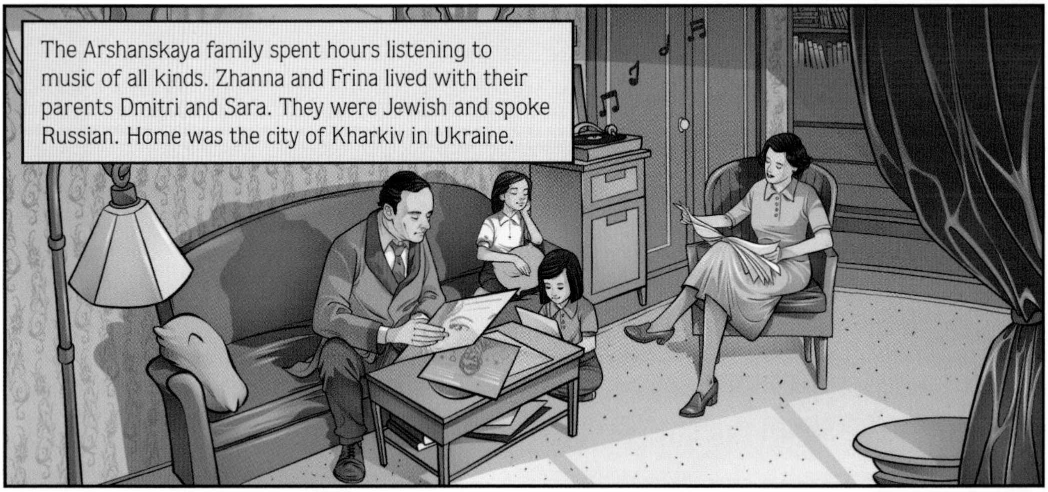
The Arshanskaya family spent hours listening to music of all kinds. Zhanna and Frina lived with their parents Dmitri and Sara. They were Jewish and spoke Russian. Home was the city of Kharkiv in Ukraine.

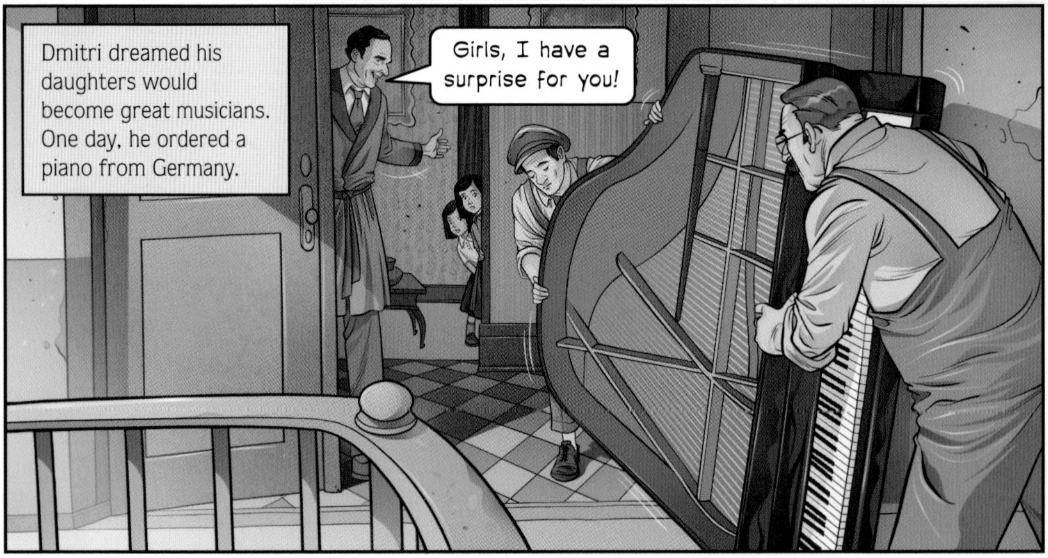
Dmitri dreamed his daughters would become great musicians. One day, he ordered a piano from Germany.
Girls, I have a surprise for you!

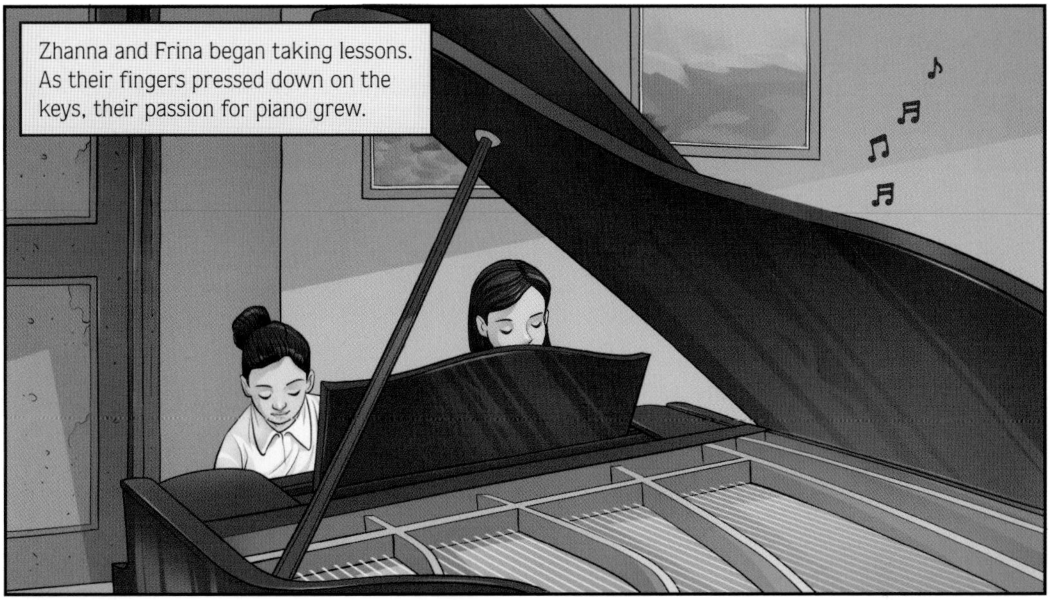
Zhanna and Frina began taking lessons. As their fingers pressed down on the keys, their passion for piano grew.

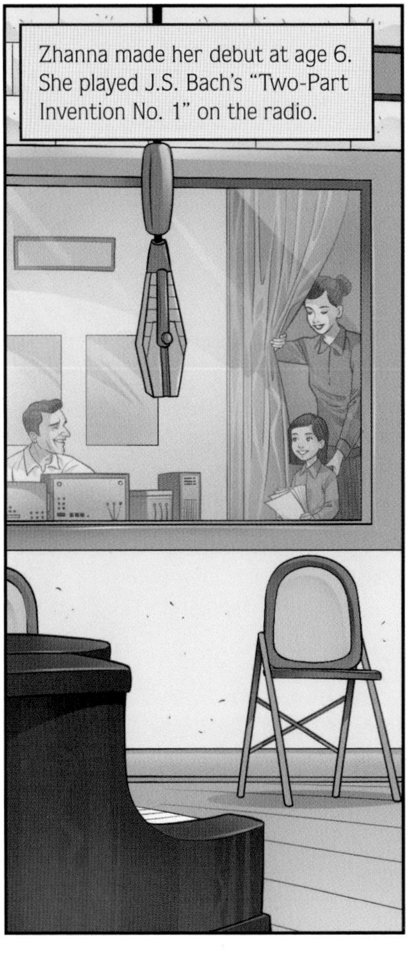
Zhanna made her debut at age 6. She played J.S. Bach's "Two-Part Invention No. 1" on the radio.

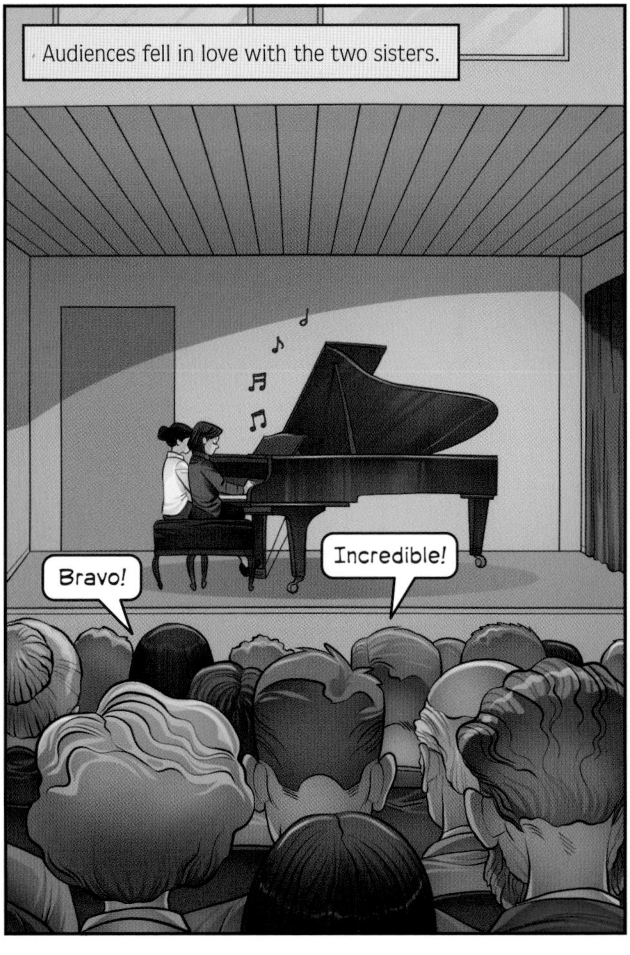
Audiences fell in love with the two sisters.
Bravo!
Incredible!

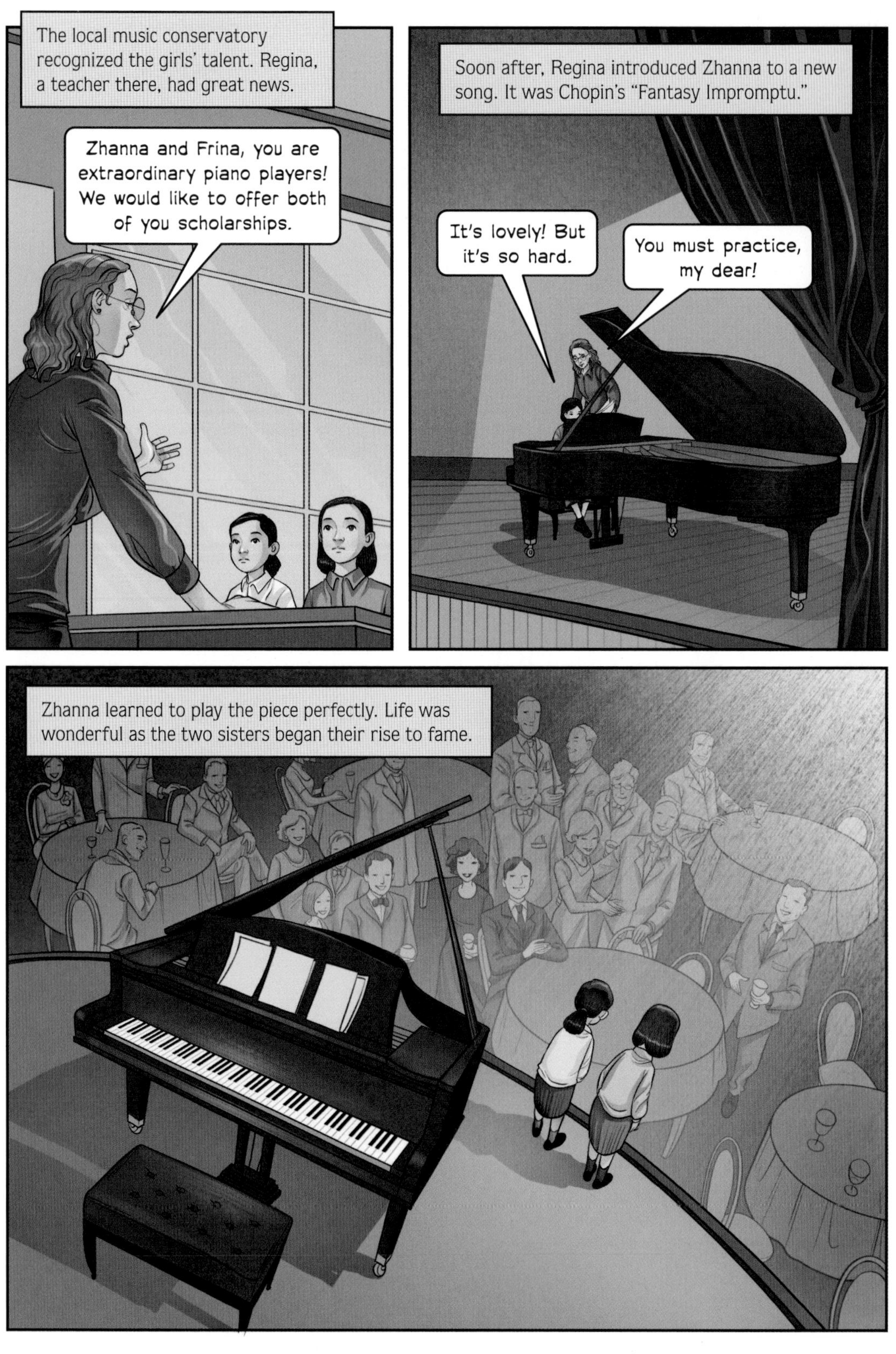
The local music conservatory recognized the girls' talent. Regina, a teacher there, had great news.
Zhanna and Frina, you are extraordinary piano players! We would like to offer both of you scholarships.
Soon after, Regina introduced Zhanna to a new song. It was Chopin's "Fantasy Impromptu."
It's lovely! But it's so hard.
You must practice, my dear!
Zhanna learned to play the piece perfectly. Life was wonderful as the two sisters began their rise to fame.

Evil Creeps In

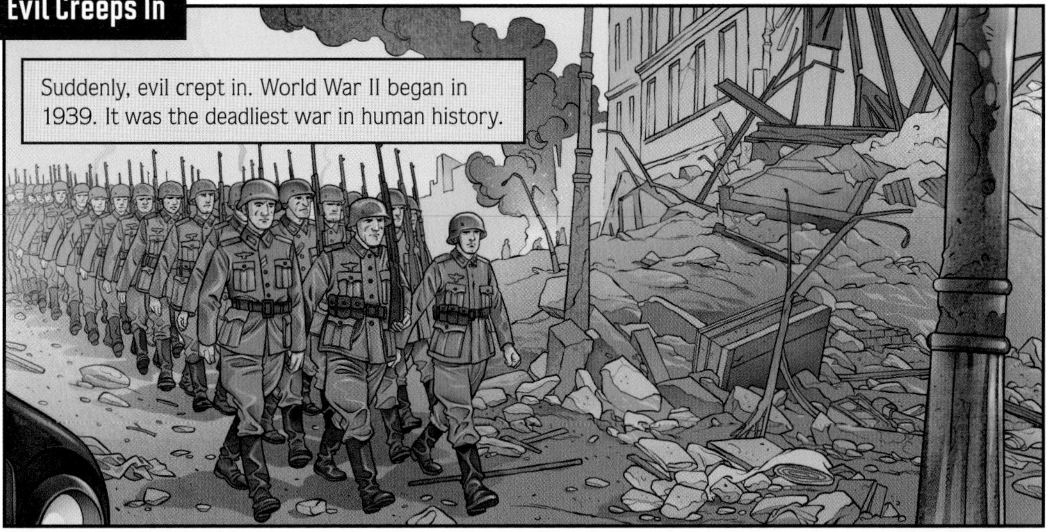
Suddenly, evil crept in. World War II began in 1939. It was the deadliest war in human history.

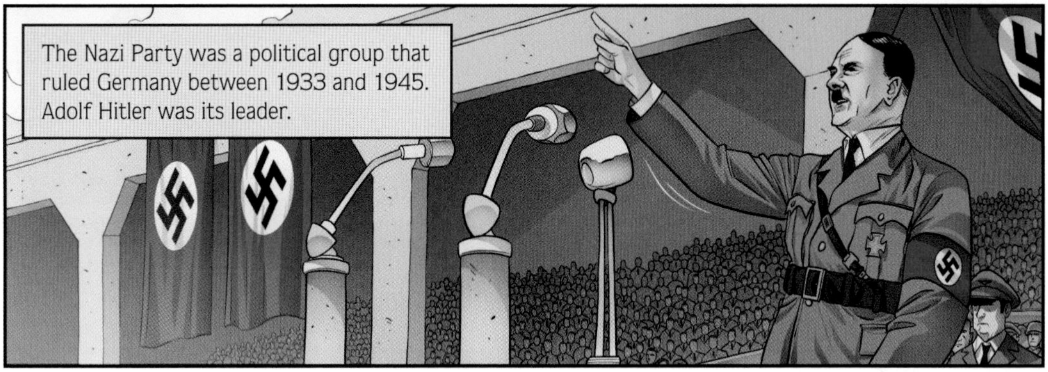
The Nazi Party was a political group that ruled Germany between 1933 and 1945. Adolf Hitler was its leader.

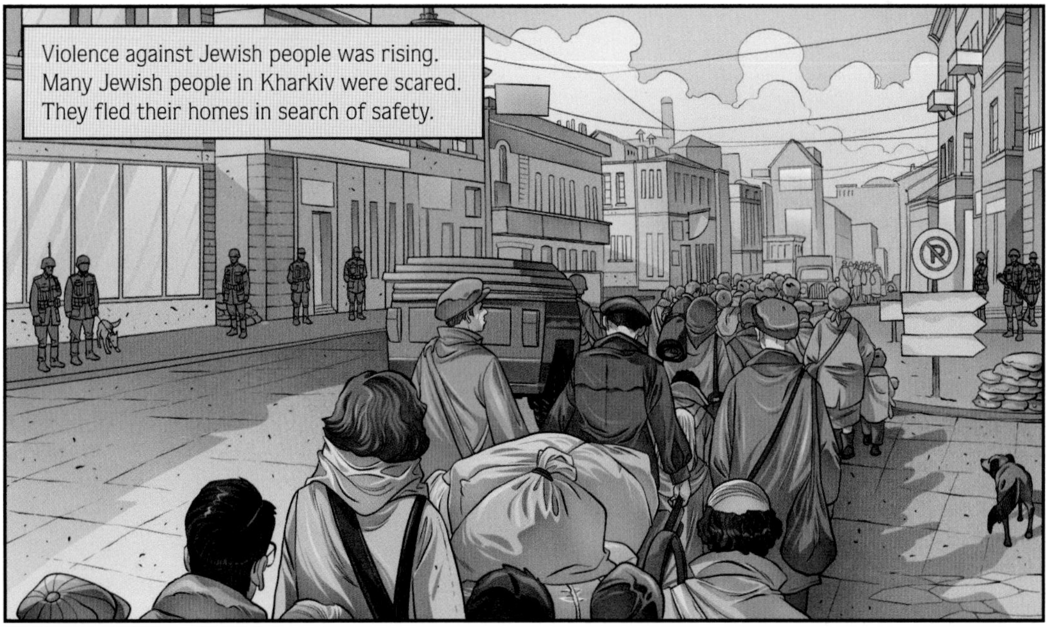
Violence against Jewish people was rising. Many Jewish people in Kharkiv were scared. They fled their homes in search of safety.

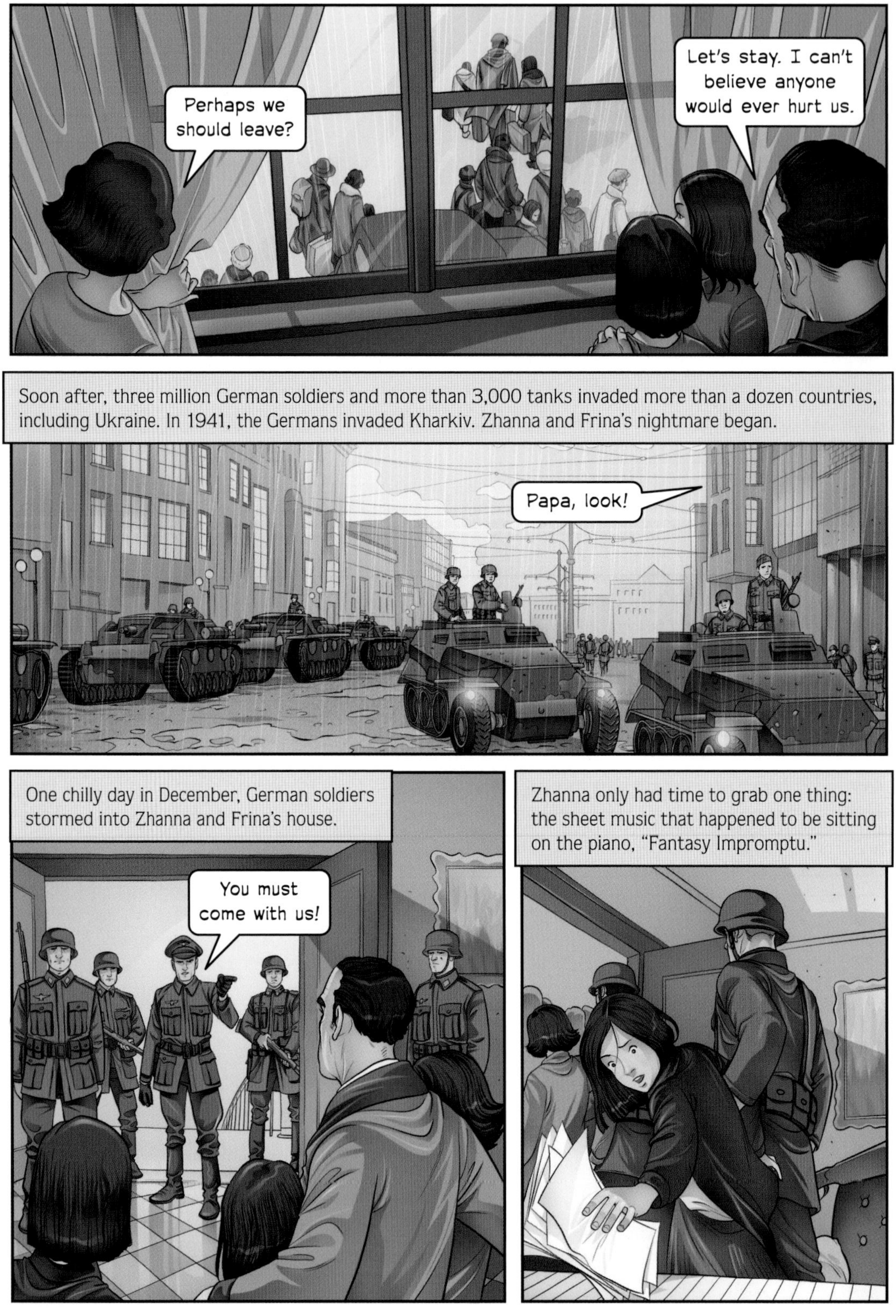
Perhaps we should leave?
Let's stay. I can't believe anyone would ever hurt us.
Soon after, three million German soldiers and more than 3,000 tanks invaded more than a dozen countries, including Ukraine. In 1941, the Germans invaded Kharkiv. Zhanna and Frina's nightmare began.
Papa, look!
One chilly day in December, German soldiers stormed into Zhanna and Frina's house.
You must come with us!
Zhanna only had time to grab one thing: the sheet music that happened to be sitting on the piano, "Fantasy Impromptu."

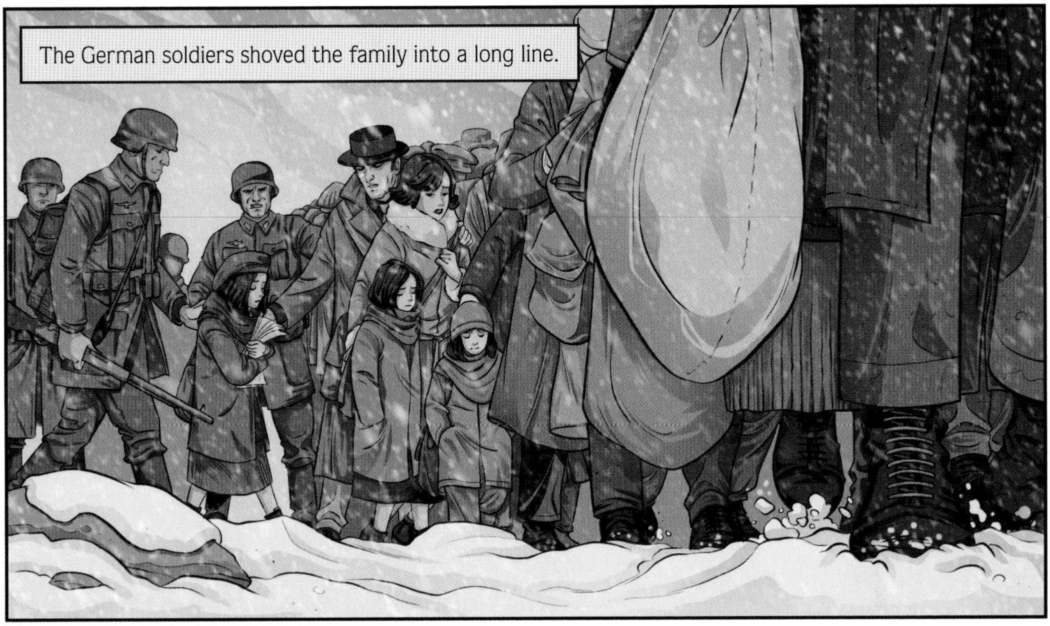
The German soldiers shoved the family into a long line.

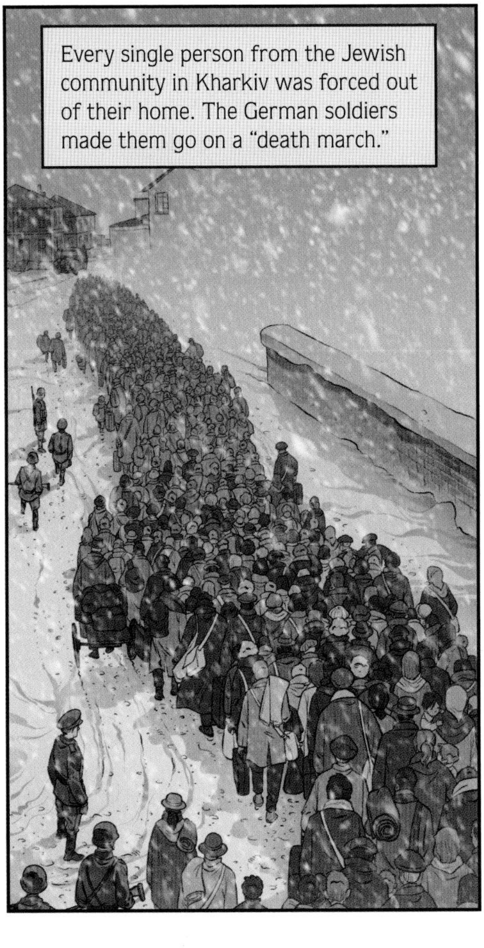
Every single person from the Jewish community in Kharkiv was forced out of their home. The German soldiers made them go on a "death march."

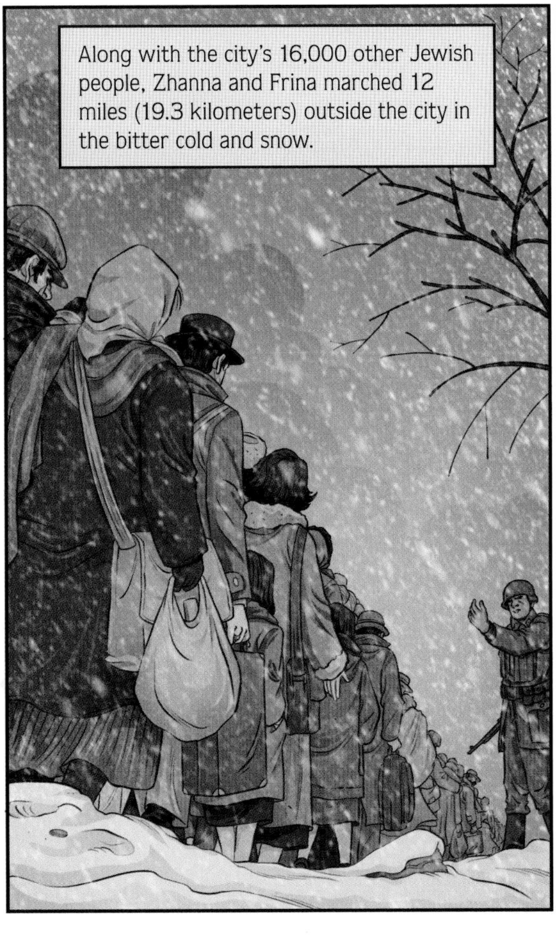
Along with the city's 16,000 other Jewish people, Zhanna and Frina marched 12 miles (19.3 kilometers) outside the city in the bitter cold and snow.

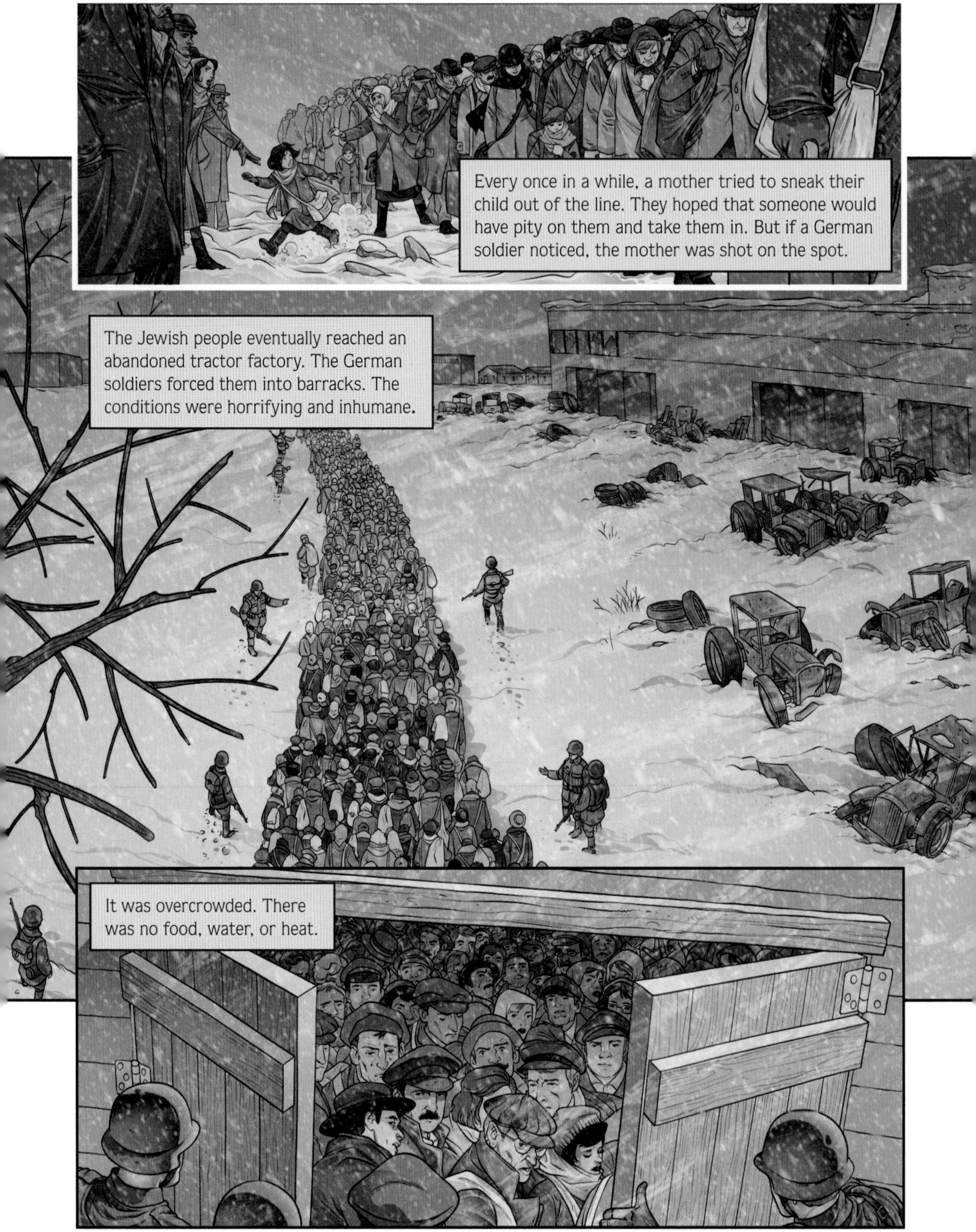
Every once in a while, a mother tried to sneak their child out of the line. They hoped that someone would have pity on them and take them in. But if a German soldier noticed, the mother was shot on the spot.
The Jewish people eventually reached an abandoned tractor factory. The German soldiers forced them into barracks. The conditions were horrifying and inhumane.
It was overcrowded. There was no food, water, or heat.

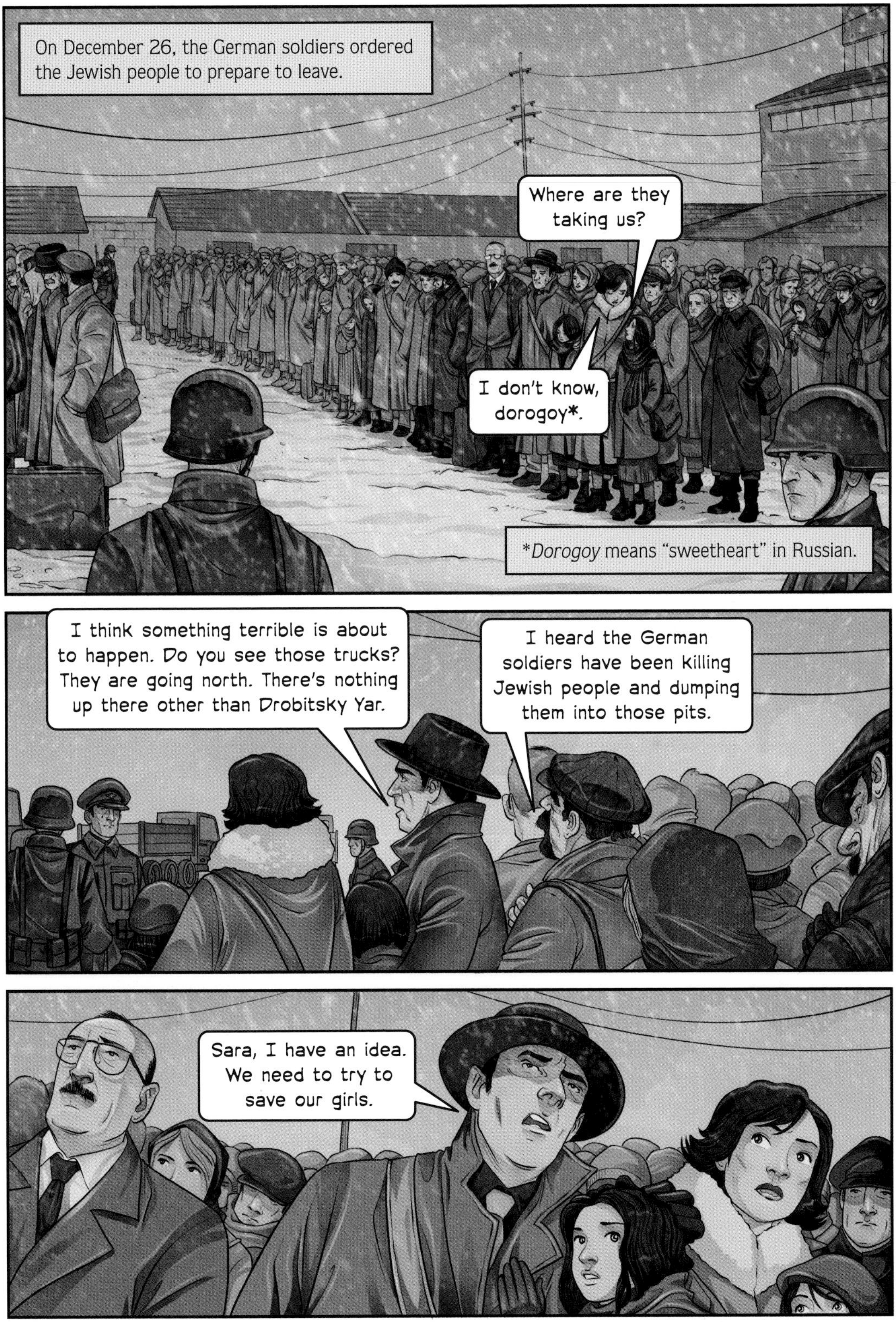
On December 26, the German soldiers ordered the Jewish people to prepare to leave.
Where are they taking us?
I don't know, dorogoy*.
*Dorogoy means "sweetheart" in Russian.
I think something terrible is about to happen. Do you see those trucks? They are going north. There's nothing up there other than Drobitsky Yar.
I heard the German soldiers have been killing Jewish people and dumping them into those pits.
Sara, I have an idea. We need to try to save our girls.

A Narrow Escape

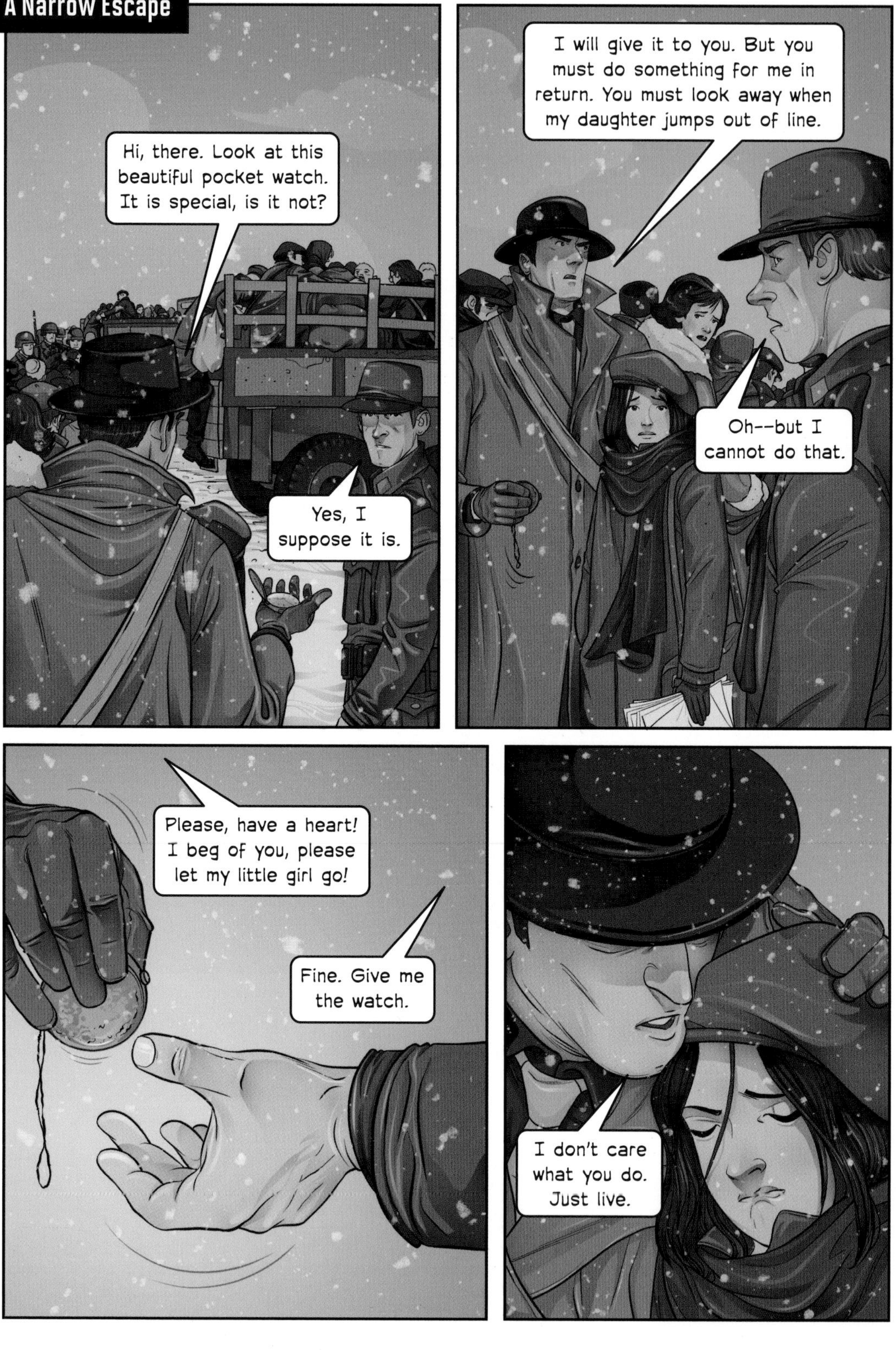
Hi, there. Look at this beautiful pocket watch. It is special, is it not?
Yes, I suppose it is.
I will give it to you. But you must do something for me in return. You must look away when my daughter jumps out of line.
Oh--but I cannot do that.
Please, have a heart! I beg of you, please let my little girl go!
Fine. Give me the watch.
I don't care what you do. Just live.

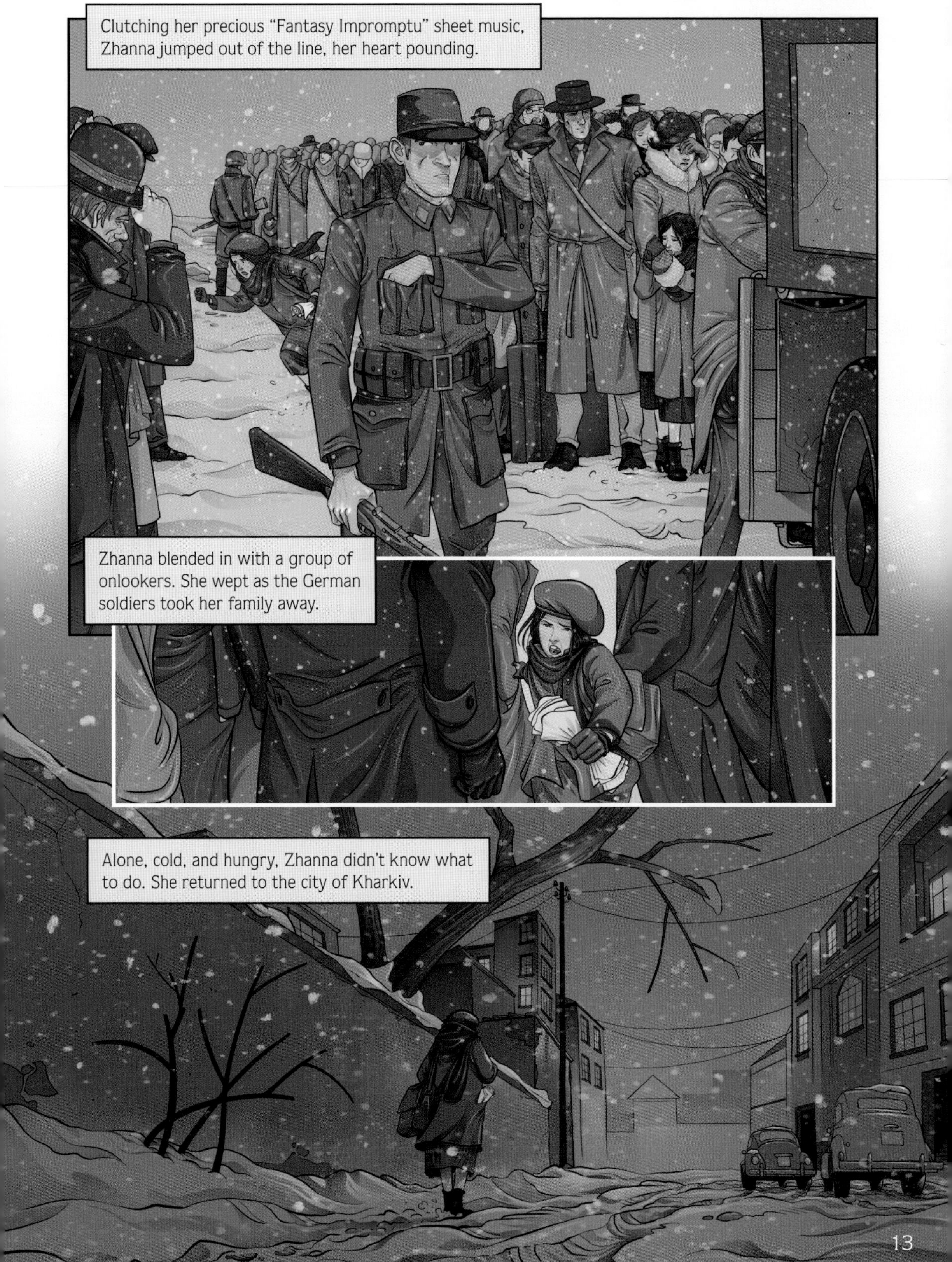
Clutching her precious "Fantasy Impromptu" sheet music, Zhanna jumped out of the line, her heart pounding.
Zhanna blended in with a group of onlookers. She wept as the German soldiers took her family away.
Alone, cold, and hungry, Zhanna didn't know what to do. She returned to the city of Kharkiv.

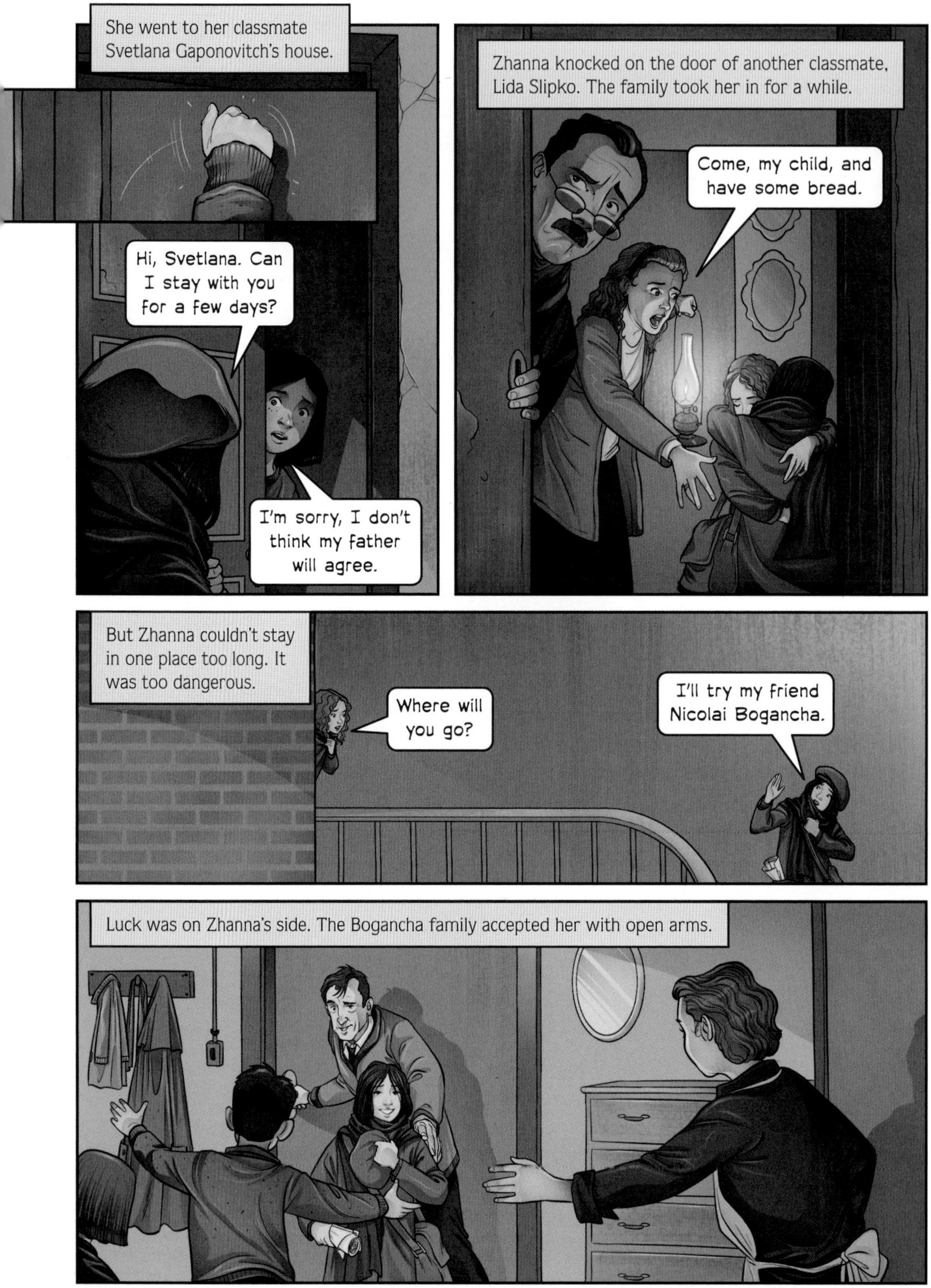
She went to her classmate Svetlana Gaponovitch's house.
Hi, Svetlana. Can I stay with you for a few days?
I'm sorry, I don't think my father will agree.
Zhanna knocked on the door of another classmate, Lida Slipko. The family took her in for a while.
Come, my child, and have some bread.
But Zhanna couldn't stay in one place too long. It was too dangerous.
Where will you go?
I'll try my friend Nicolai Bogancha.
Luck was on Zhanna's side. The Bogancha family accepted her with open arms.

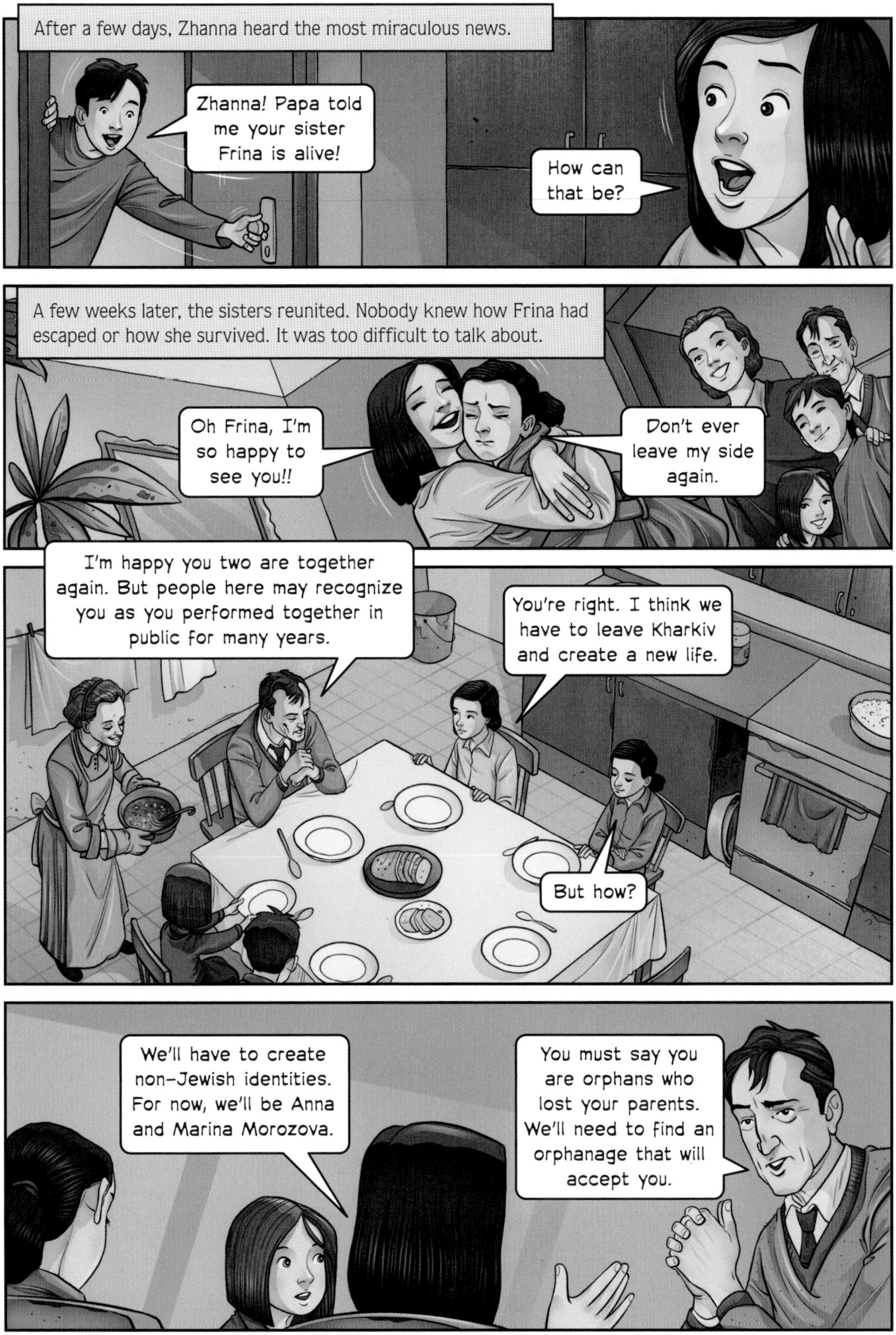
After a few days, Zhanna heard the most miraculous news.
Zhanna! Papa told me your sister Frina is alive!
How can that be?
A few weeks later, the sisters reunited. Nobody knew how Frina had escaped or how she survived. It was too difficult to talk about.
Oh Frina, I'm so happy to see you!!
Don't ever leave my side again.
I'm happy you two are together again. But people here may recognize you as you performed together in public for many years.
You're right. I think we have to leave Kharkiv and create a new life.
But how?
We'll have to create non-Jewish identities. For now, we'll be Anna and Marina Morozova.
You must say you are orphans who lost your parents. We'll need to find an orphanage that will accept you.

Shoved into the Limelight

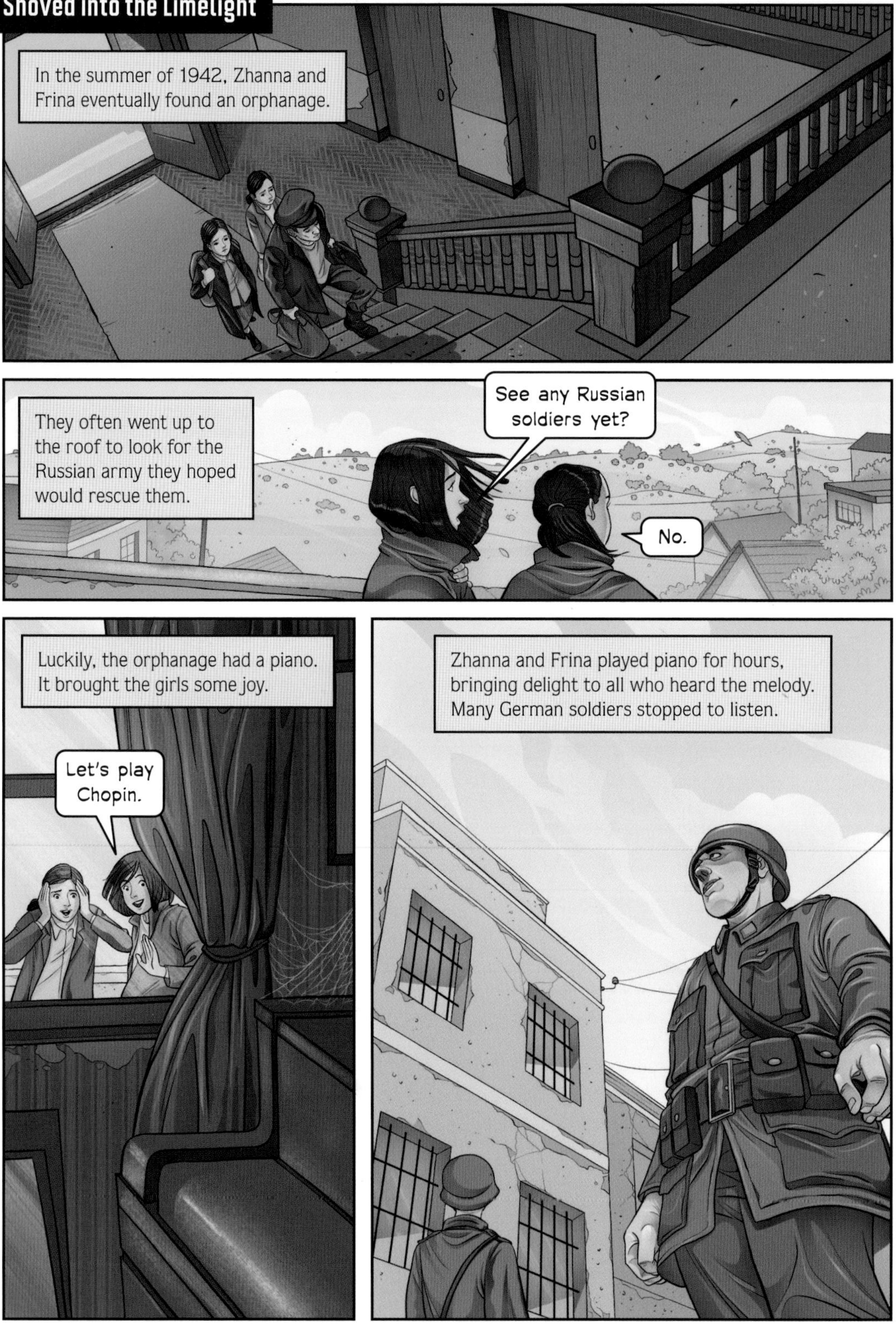
In the summer of 1942, Zhanna and Frina eventually found an orphanage.
They often went up to the roof to look for the Russian army they hoped would rescue them.
See any Russian soldiers yet?
No.
Luckily, the orphanage had a piano. It brought the girls some joy.
Let's play Chopin.
Zhanna and Frina played piano for hours, bringing delight to all who heard the melody. Many German soldiers stopped to listen.

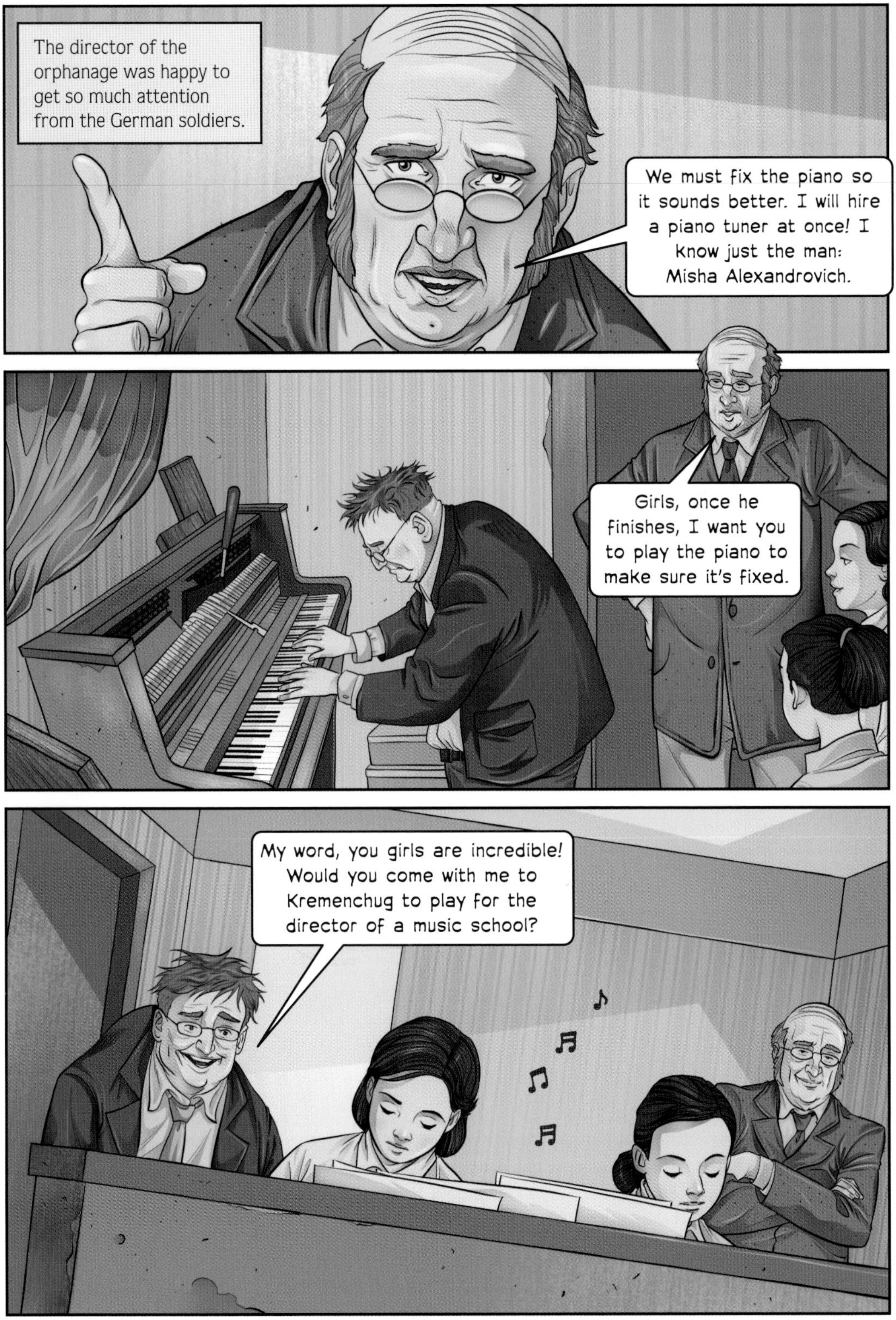
The director of the orphanage was happy to get so much attention from the German soldiers.
We must fix the piano so it sounds better. I will hire a piano tuner at once! I know just the man: Misha Alexandrovich.
Girls, once he finishes, I want you to play the piano to make sure it's fixed.
My word, you girls are incredible! Would you come with me to Kremenchug to play for the director of a music school?

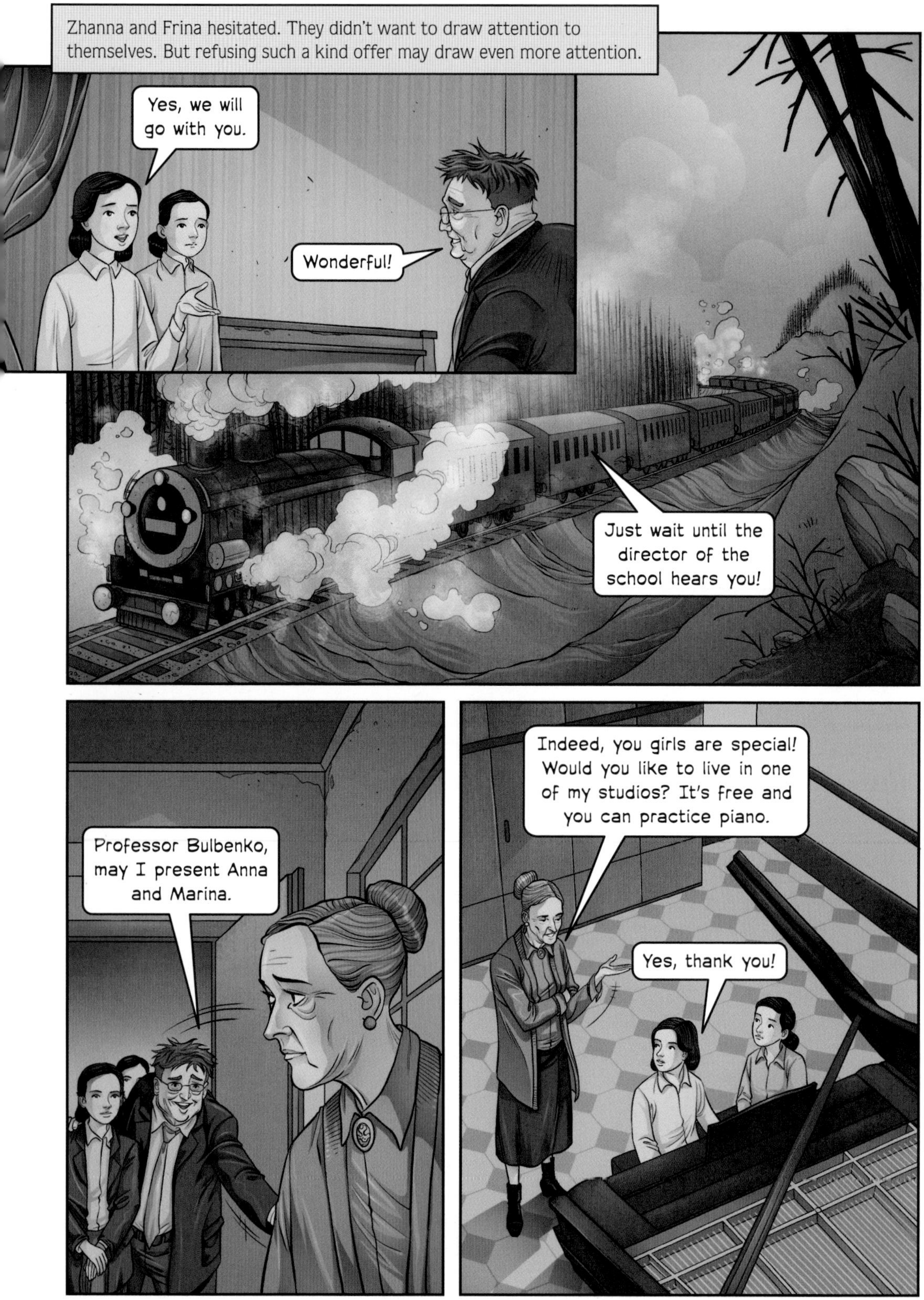

Zhanna and Frina hesitated. They didn't want to draw attention to themselves. But refusing such a kind offer may draw even more attention.
Yes, we will go with you.
Wonderful!
Just wait until the director of the school hears you!
Professor Bulbenko, may I present Anna and Marina.
Indeed, you girls are special! Would you like to live in one of my studios? It's free and you can practice piano.
Yes, thank you!

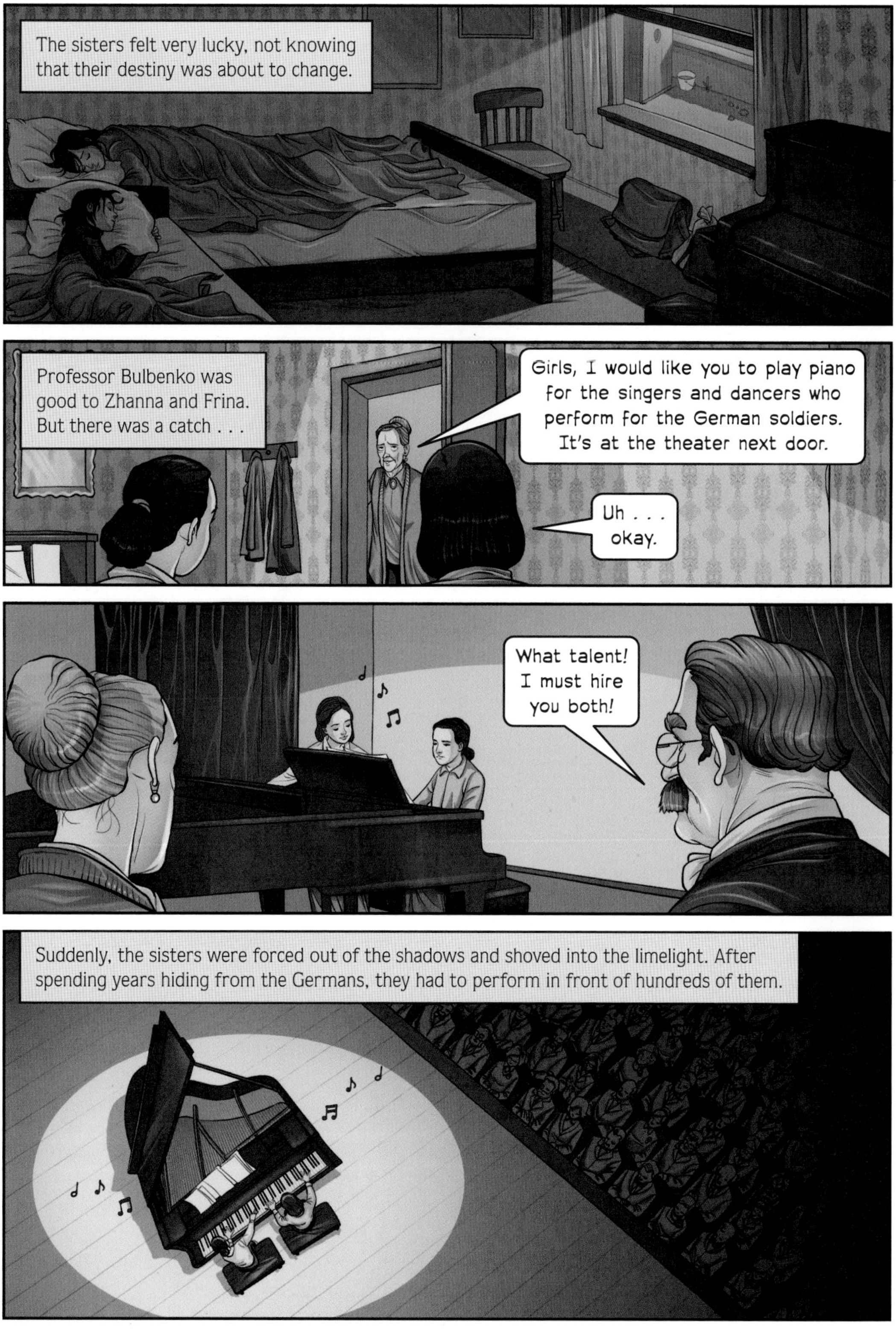
The sisters felt very lucky, not knowing that their destiny was about to change.
Professor Bulbenko was good to Zhanna and Frina. But there was a catch . . .
Girls, I would like you to play piano for the singers and dancers who perform for the German soldiers. It's at the theater next door.
Uh . . . okay.
What talent! I must hire you both!
Suddenly, the sisters were forced out of the shadows and shoved into the limelight. After spending years hiding from the Germans, they had to perform in front of hundreds of them.

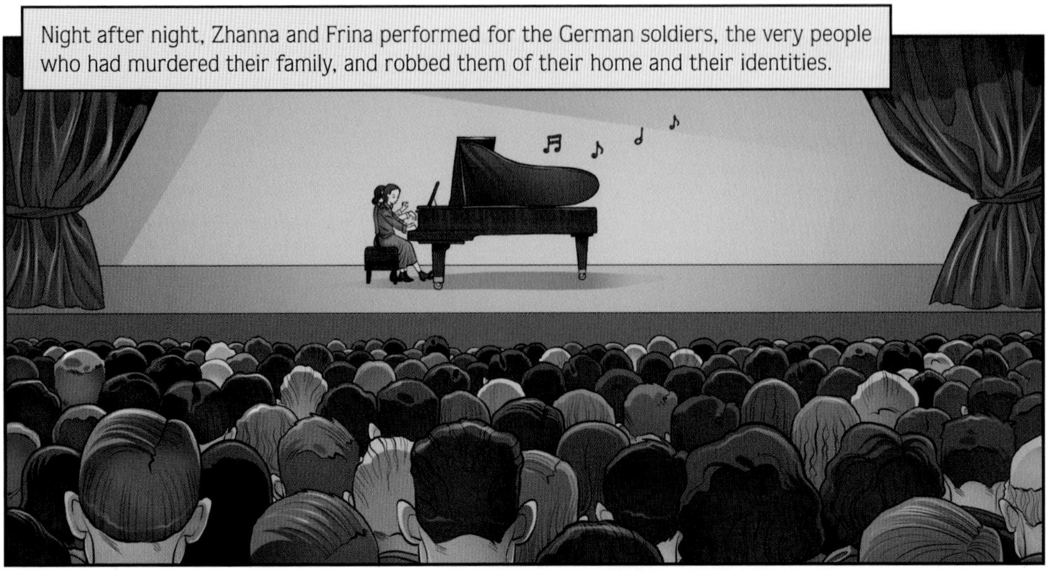
Night after night, Zhanna and Frina performed for the German soldiers, the very people who had murdered their family, and robbed them of their home and their identities.

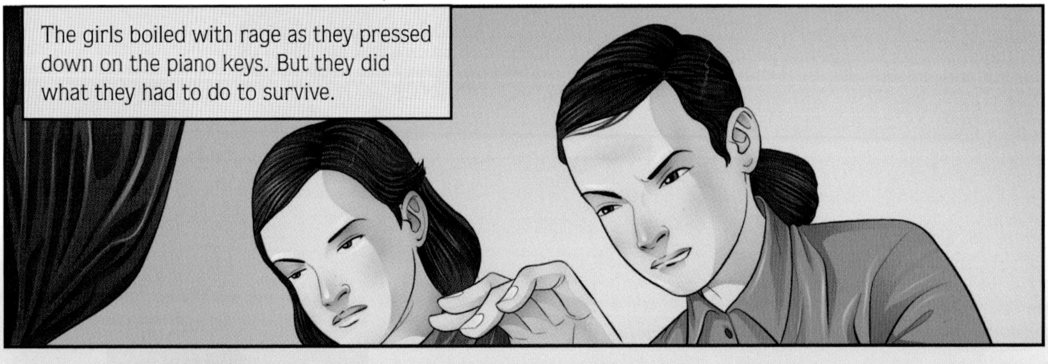
The girls boiled with rage as they pressed down on the piano keys. But they did what they had to do to survive.

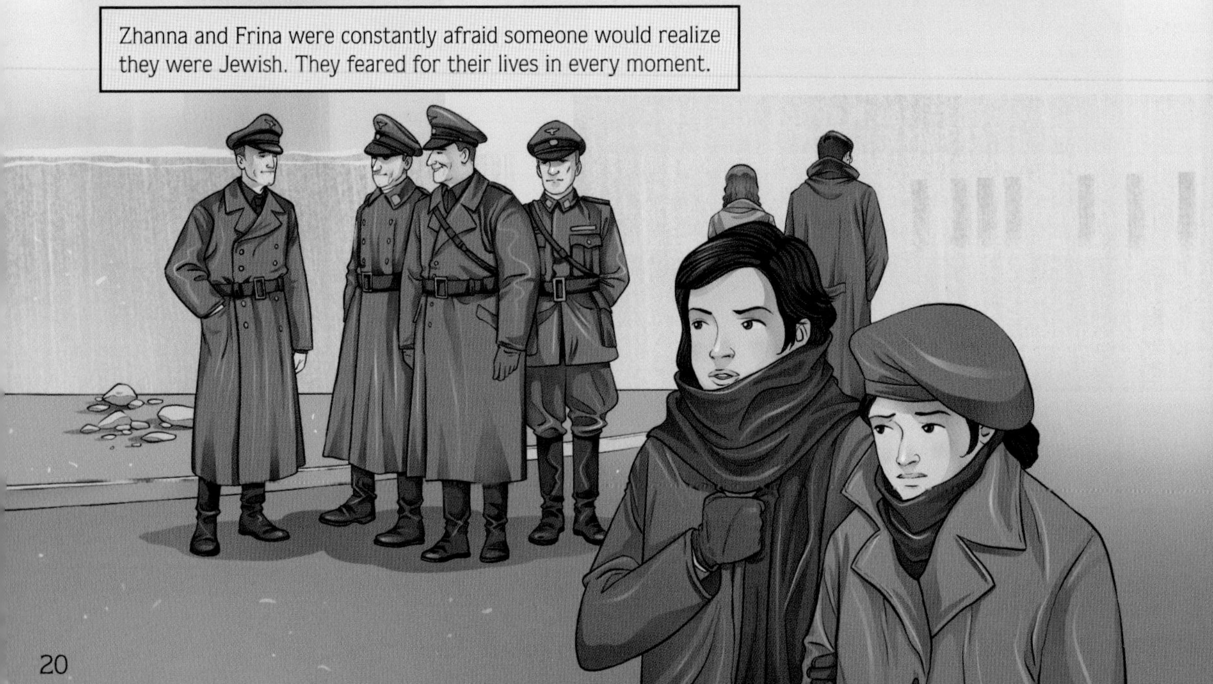
Zhanna and Frina were constantly afraid someone would realize they were Jewish. They feared for their lives in every moment.

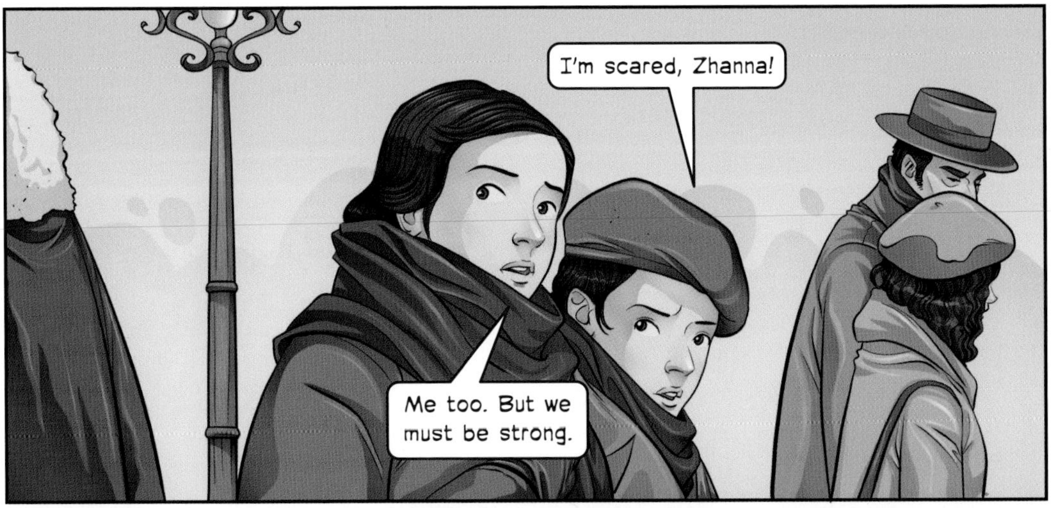
I'm scared, Zhanna!
Me too. But we must be strong.

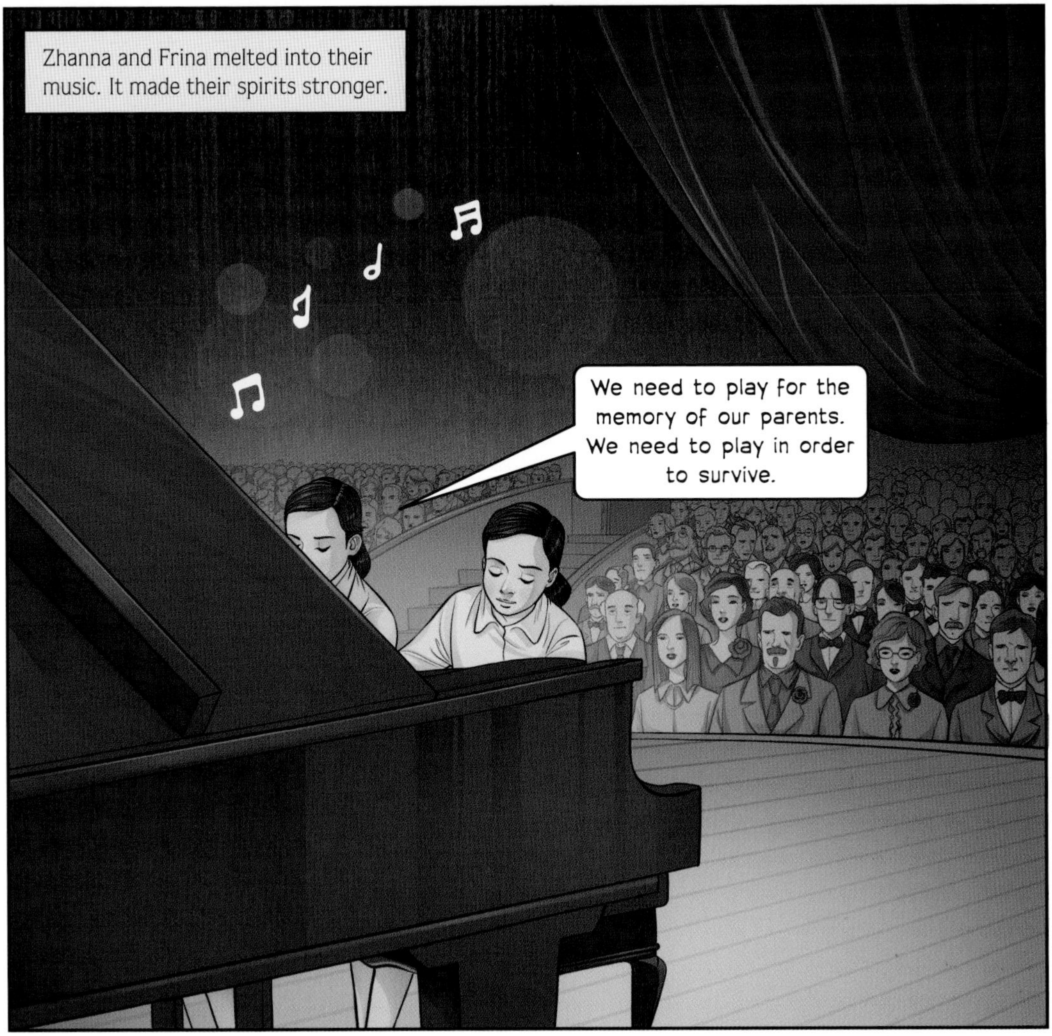
Zhanna and Frina melted into their music. It made their spirits stronger.
We need to play for the memory of our parents. We need to play in order to survive.

Forging a New Path

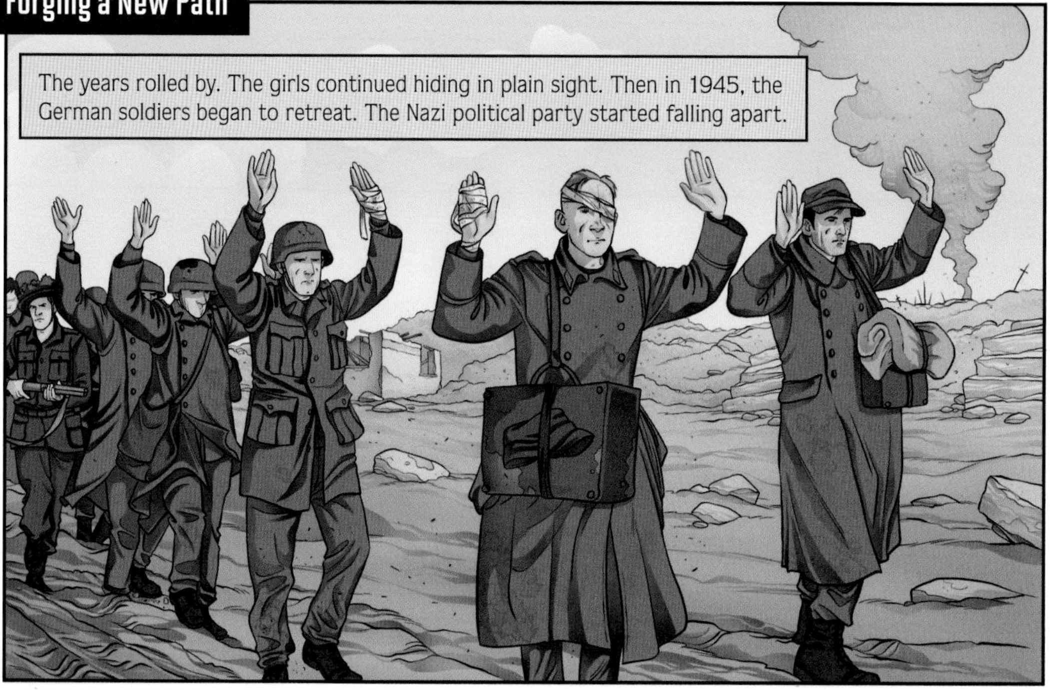
The years rolled by. The girls continued hiding in plain sight. Then in 1945, the German soldiers began to retreat. The Nazi political party started falling apart.

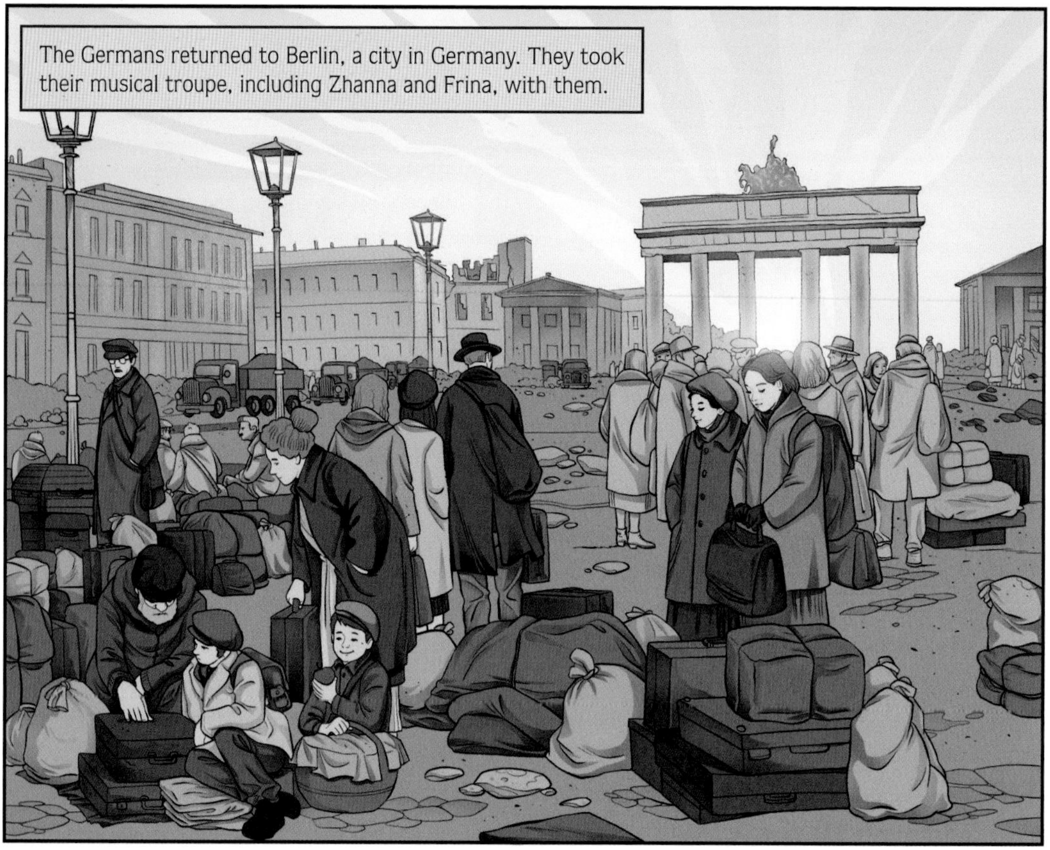
The Germans returned to Berlin, a city in Germany. They took their musical troupe, including Zhanna and Frina, with them.

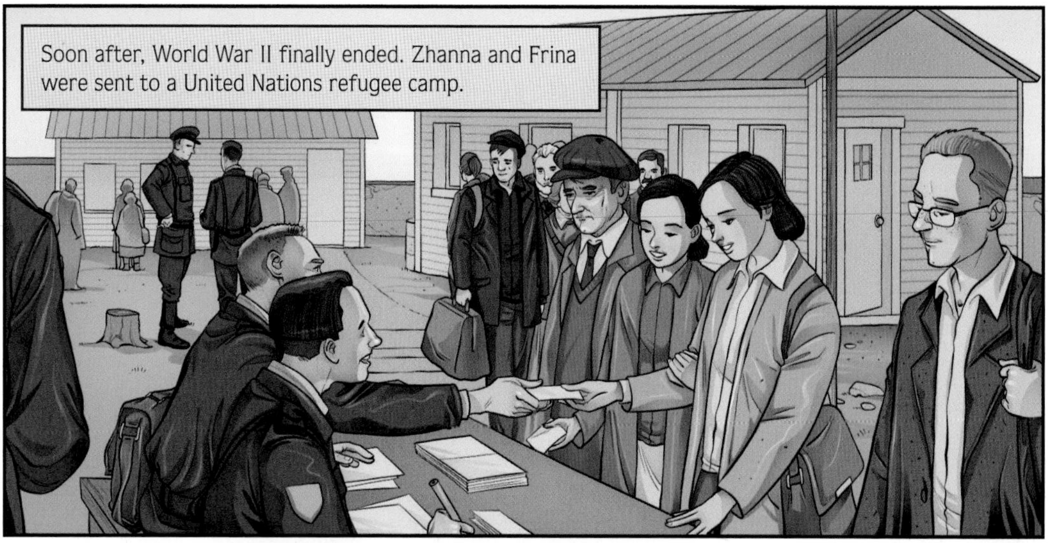
Soon after, World War II finally ended. Zhanna and Frina were sent to a United Nations refugee camp.

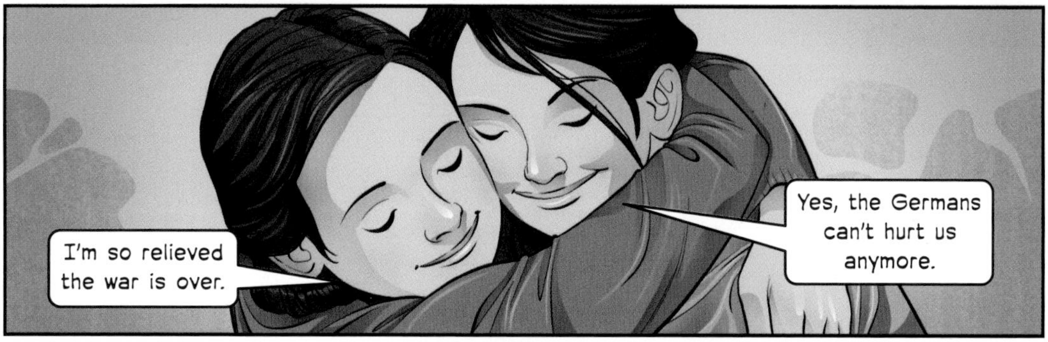
I'm so relieved the war is over.
Yes, the Germans can't hurt us anymore.

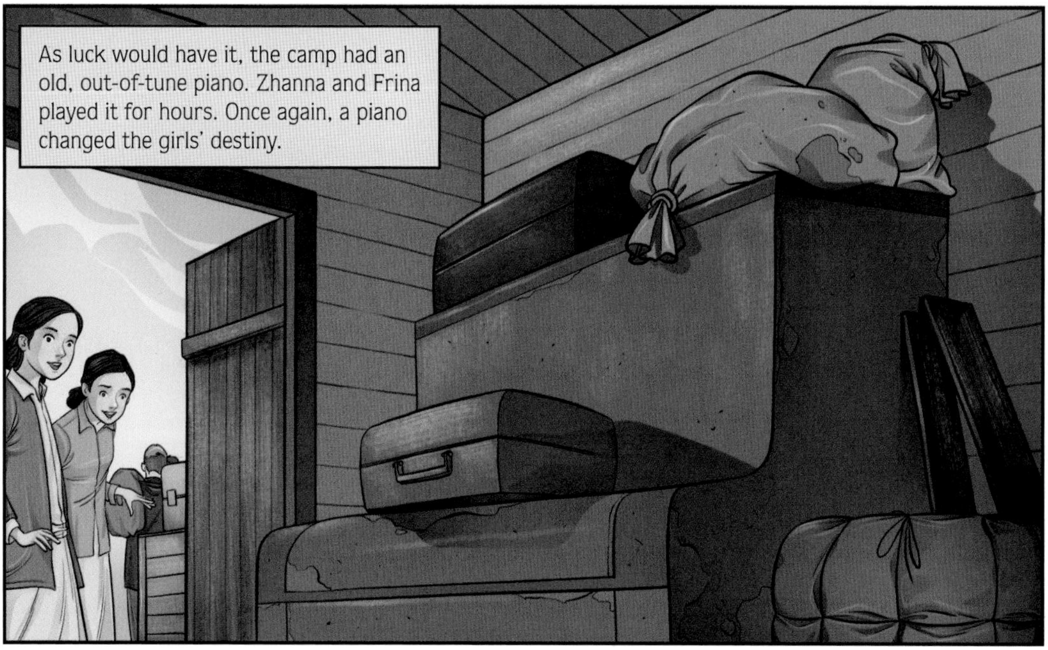
As luck would have it, the camp had an old, out-of-tune piano. Zhanna and Frina played it for hours. Once again, a piano changed the girls' destiny.

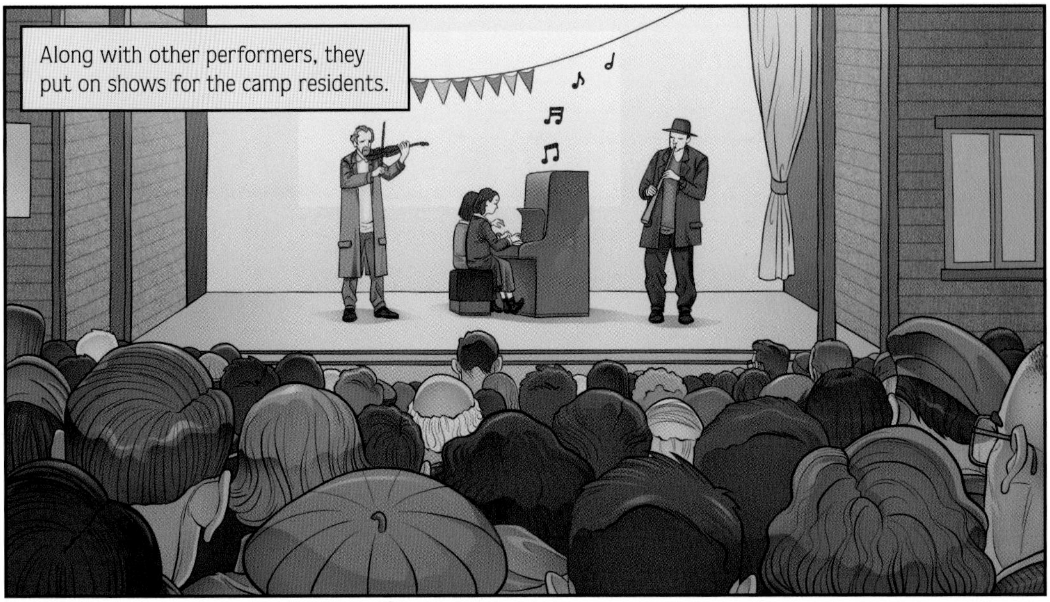
Along with other performers, they put on shows for the camp residents.

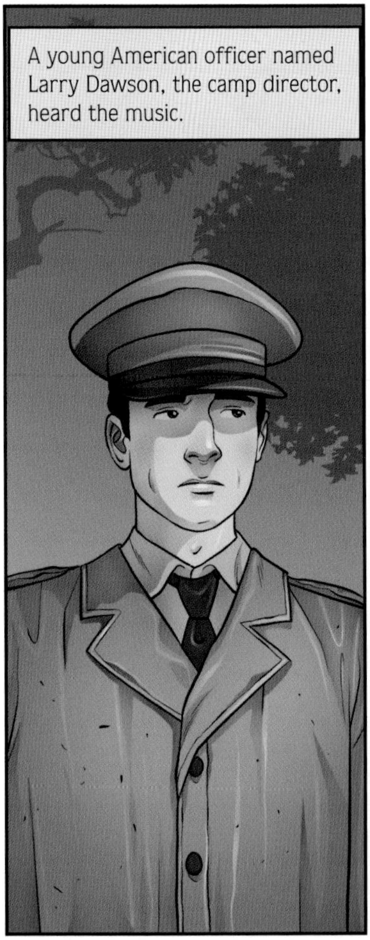
A young American officer named Larry Dawson, the camp director, heard the music.

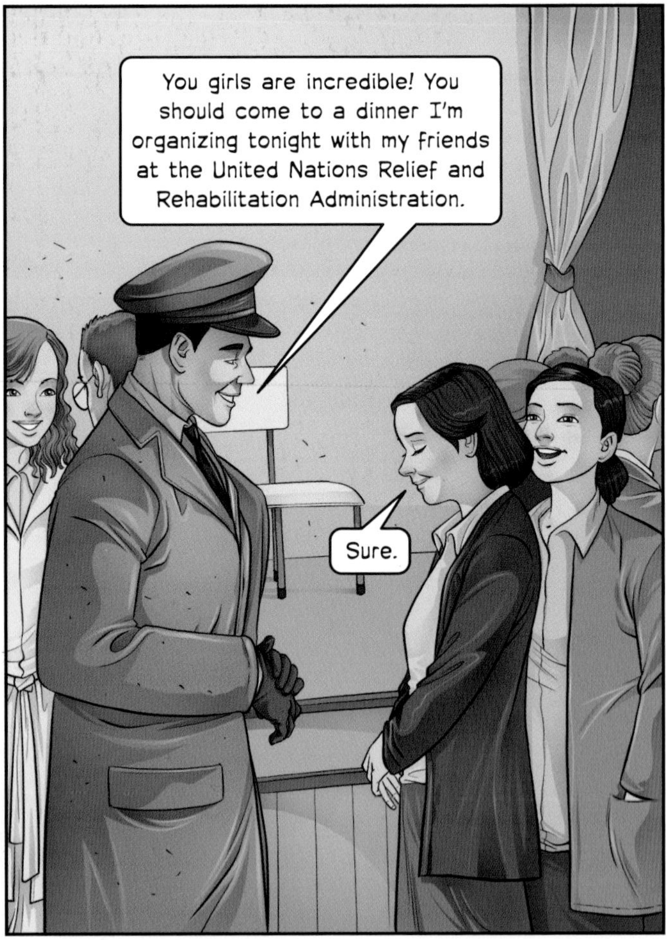
You girls are incredible! You should come to a dinner I'm organizing tonight with my friends at the United Nations Relief and Rehabilitation Administration.
Sure.

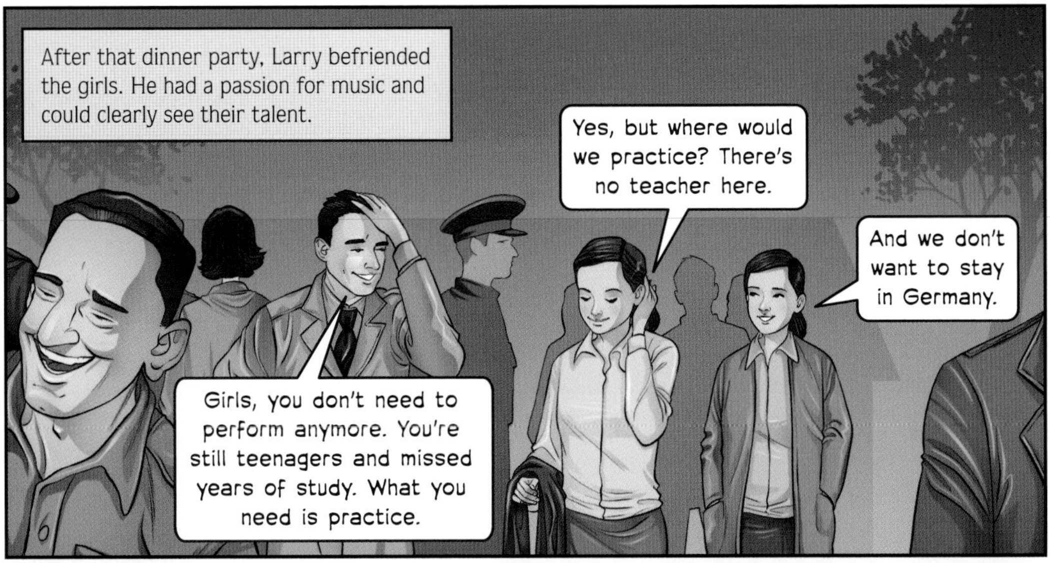
After that dinner party, Larry befriended the girls. He had a passion for music and could clearly see their talent.
Girls, you don't need to perform anymore. You're still teenagers and missed years of study. What you need is practice.
Yes, but where would we practice? There's no teacher here.
And we don't want to stay in Germany.

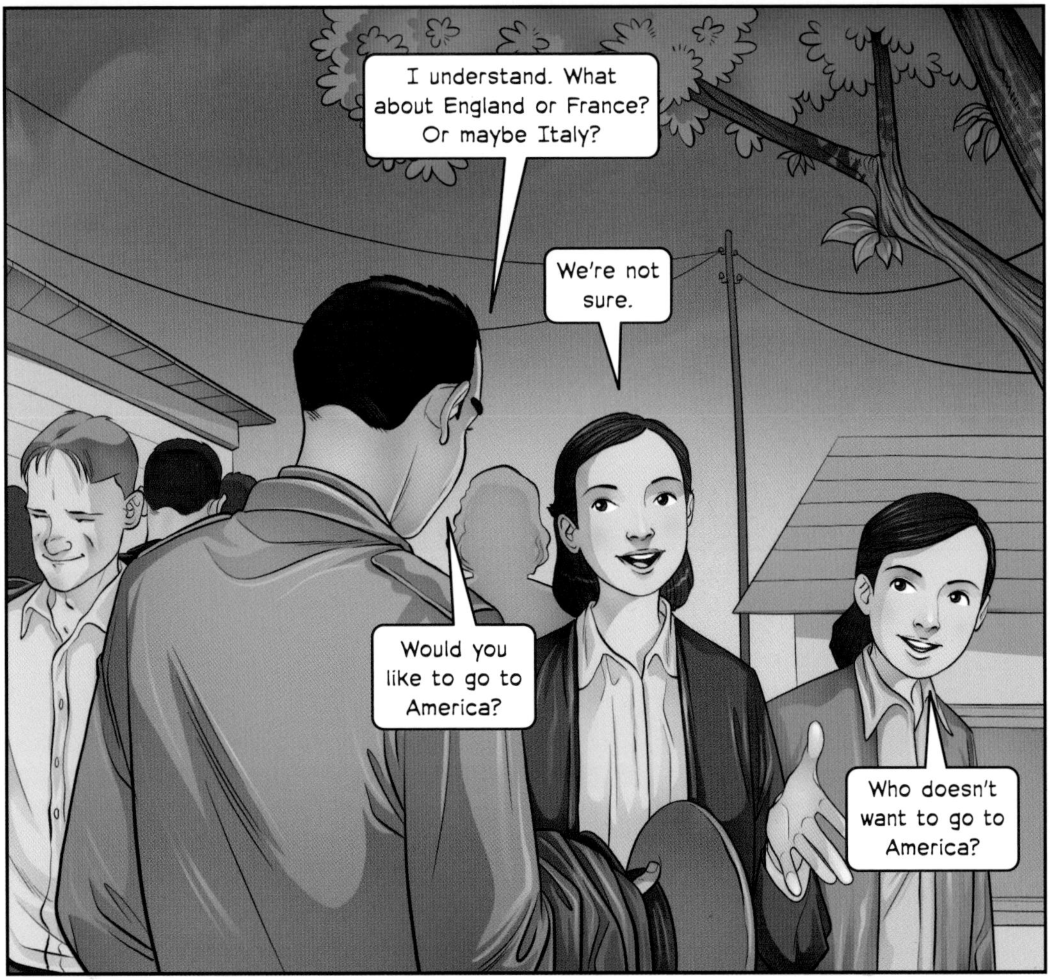
I understand. What about England or France? Or maybe Italy?
We're not sure.
Would you like to go to America?
Who doesn't want to go to America?

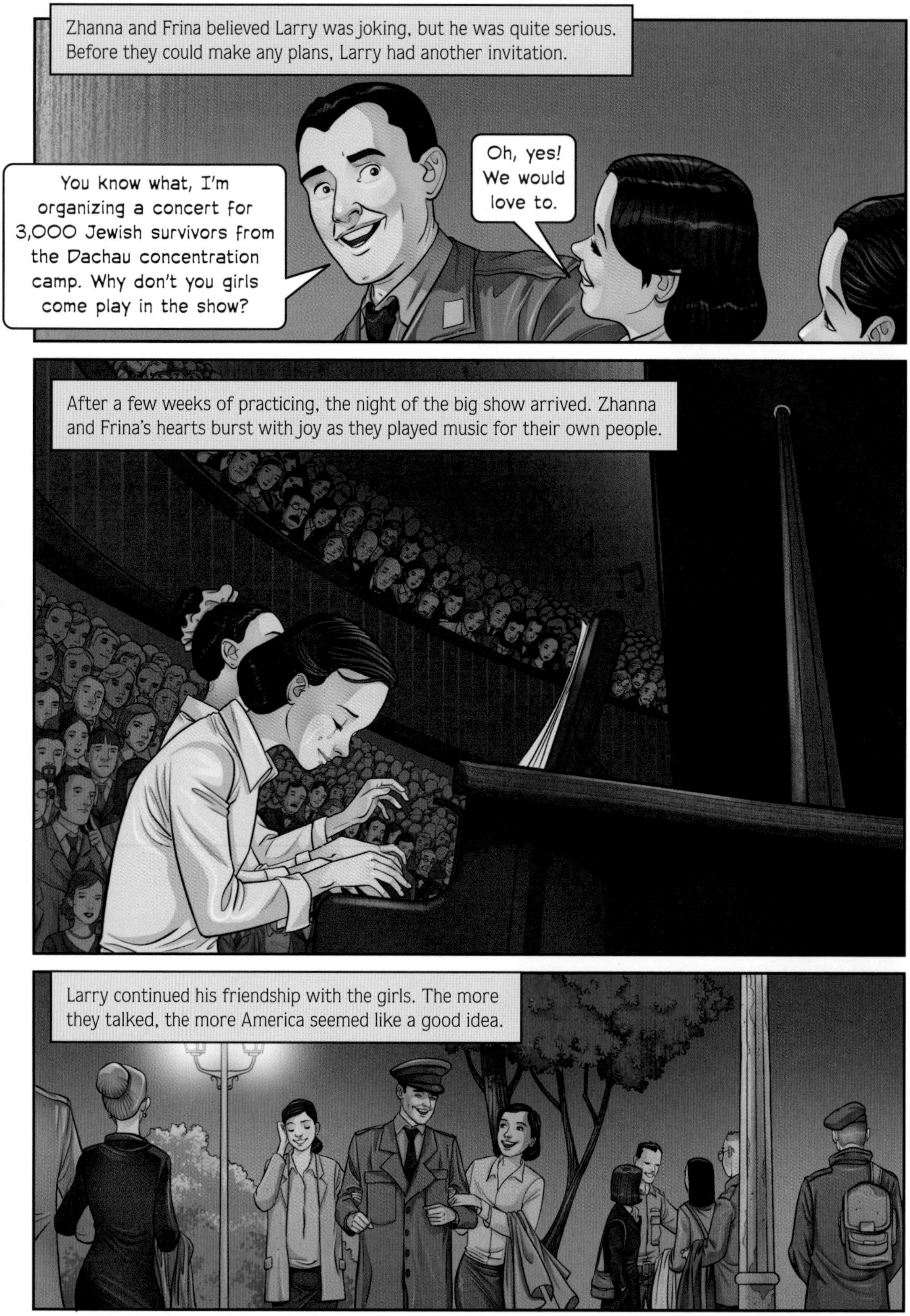
Zhanna and Frina believed Larry was joking, but he was quite serious. Before they could make any plans, Larry had another invitation.
You know what, I'm organizing a concert for 3,000 Jewish survivors from the Dachau concentration camp. Why don't you girls come play in the show?
Oh, yes! We would love to.
After a few weeks of practicing, the night of the big show arrived. Zhanna and Frina's hearts burst with joy as they played music for their own people.
Larry continued his friendship with the girls. The more they talked, the more America seemed like a good idea.

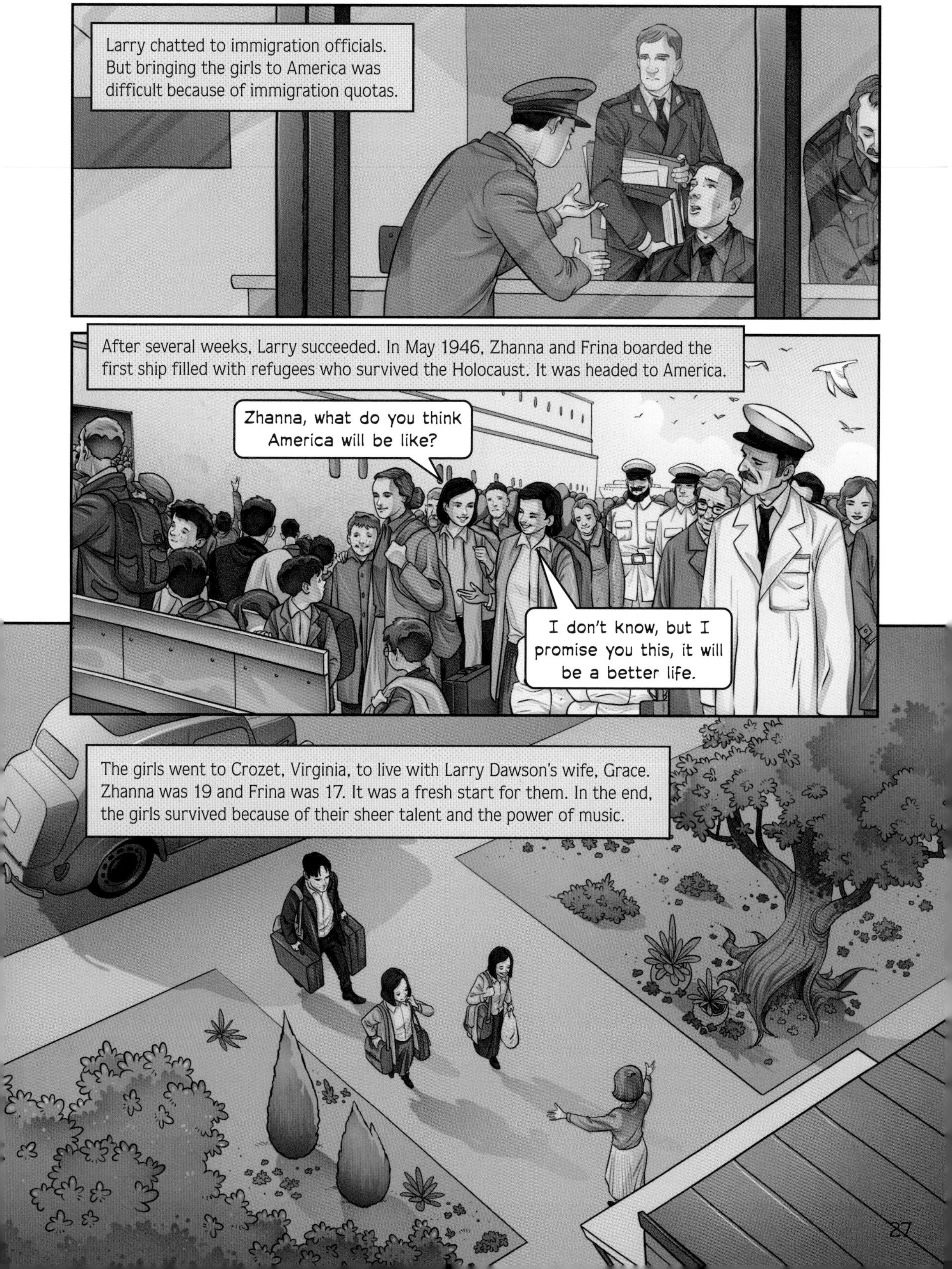
Larry chatted to immigration officials. But bringing the girls to America was difficult because of immigration quotas.
After several weeks, Larry succeeded. In May 1946, Zhanna and Frina boarded the first ship filled with refugees who survived the Holocaust. It was headed to America.
Zhanna, what do you think America will be like?
I don't know, but I promise you this, it will be a better life.
The girls went to Crozet, Virginia, to live with Larry Dawson's wife, Grace. Zhanna was 19 and Frina was 17. It was a fresh start for them. In the end, the girls survived because of their sheer talent and the power of music.

MORE ABOUT ZHANNA AND FRINA ARSHANSKAYA

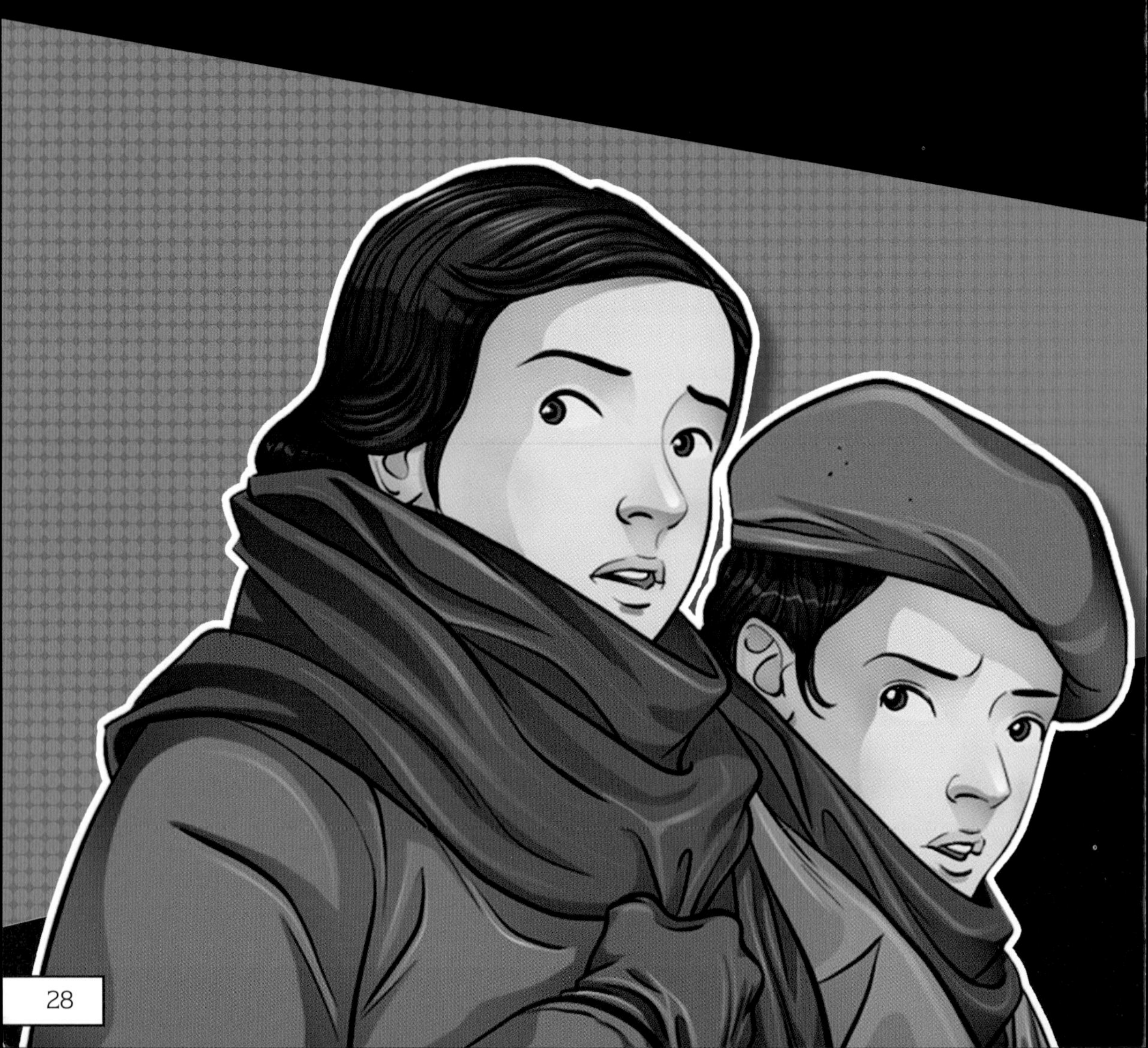

- When Zhanna and Frina arrived in the United States on May 21, 1946, their talent brought them many opportunities. They auditioned for Reginald Stewart, the director of the Peabody Conservatory. Reginald offered them scholarships right away. Zhanna and Frina were happy, but Larry Dawson felt they could do better. He eventually got them an audition for the world-famous school of Juilliard, where they both won scholarships.

- Soon after, Zhanna fell in love with violist David Dawson, Larry's brother. They got married and moved to Bloomington, Indiana. They joined the music faculty at Indiana University and raised two sons together.

- Frina eventually married pianist Kenwyn Boldt. They both worked at the State University of New York in Buffalo.

- Zhanna's sons never knew that their mother survived the Holocaust. She didn't want them reliving her pain. Her son Greg Dawson didn't even know he was Jewish until he was an adult. In the spring of 1978, he worked as a reporter for the Bloomington newspaper. At the time, they were producing a series about the Holocaust. Greg wanted to write an article and asked his mother to tell him about her memories as a Russian who lived through the war. Greg traveled to Ukraine to do more research. Much to his surprise, he saw his mother and aunt's names listed on the memorial tomb for the victims of Kharkiv. Greg pieced the story together and wrote the book *Hiding in the Spotlight: A Musical Prodigy's Story of Survival, 1941–1946*.

- Greg believes his mother and aunt are the only two Jewish survivors from Kharkiv. Nobody knew their story for decades, but now thanks to his book and the interviews and articles that followed, the world learned about Zhanna and Frina, two young girls who, against all odds, persevered and used music as a way to survive a horrifying situation.

GLOSSARY

barracks (BEH-ruhks)—a building or set of buildings used as a living space, usually by soldiers

concentration camp (kon-suhn-TRAY-shuhn KAMP)—a place with terrible living conditions where many people (in this case, Jewish people) are imprisoned and later killed

debut (day-BYOO)—a person's first performance

destiny (DES-tuh-nee)—the events that will happen to a particular person or thing in the future

immigration quota (im-i-GRAY-shuhn KWOH-tuh)—when a country limits the number of immigrants allowed to enter that country each year (an immigrant is a person living in a country other than that of his or her birth)

inhumane (in-hyoo-MAYN)—cruel, without any compassion

invade (in-VAYD)—when soldiers enter a region with the goal of taking over

music conservatory (MYOO-zik kuhn-SUR-vuh-tawr-ee)—a school for education in musical performance and composition

Nazi (NAHT-see)—a member of the National Socialist German Workers' Party, the political party founded by Adolf Hitler in Germany

refugee (ref-yoo-JEE)—a person who has been forced to leave their country in order to escape a terrible situation like war

retreat (ri-TREET)—when someone (in this case, an army) withdraws or leaves a region they took over

scholarship (SKOL-er-ship)—an award given to a student that pays for some or all of their education at a particular school, based on their achievements

READ MORE

Herman, Gail. *What Was the Holocaust?* New York: Penguin Workshop, 2018.

Shackleton, Kath, editor. *Survivors of the Holocaust*. Naperville, IL: Sourcebooks eXplore, 2019.

Vilardi, Debbie. *Anne Frank Writes Words of Hope: Courageous Kid of World War II*. North Mankato, MN: Capstone Press, 2023.

INTERNET SITES

The Life of Anne Frank
natgeokids.com/uk/discover/history/general-history/anne-frank-facts/

World War II
historyforkids.net/world-war-two.html

World War II: The Holocaust
ducksters.com/history/world_war_ii/holocaust.php

ABOUT THE AUTHOR

Lydia Lukidis is passionate about history, mythology, and science. She's the author of more than 50 trade and educational books such as *Dancing through Space: Dr. Mae Jemison Soars to New Heights*; *Deep, Deep, Down: The Secret Underwater Poetry of the Mariana Trench*; and *The Broken Bees' Nest*, which was nominated for a Cybils Award. Lydia also helps foster children's literacy and offers writing workshops and author visits in elementary schools. She lives in Montreal, Quebec, with her lovely daughter. They both love reading and writing!

ABOUT THE ILLUSTRATOR

Aleksandar Sotirovski was born in Bitola, Yugoslavia. He is a Macedonian illustrator and comic artist with decades of international experience. He has published his works all around the world for a variety of book and comic publishers. He has also produced concepts for several German and American video game companies, storyboards for featured films, and more than 300 advertisements.